D1405834

The Joy Choice

©1994 by Elizabeth B. Brown

Published by Fleming H. Revell
a division of Baker Book House Company
P.O. Box 6287, Grand Rapids, MI 49516-6287

Printed in the United States of America

All rights reserved. No part of this publication may be reproduced, stored in a retrieval system, or transmitted in any form or by any means—electronic, mechanical, photocopy, recording, or any other—without the prior written permission of the publisher. The only exception is brief quotations in printed reviews.

Library of Congress Cataloging-in-Publication Data

Brown, Elizabeth B.
   The joy choice : happiness is an inside job / Elizabeth B. Brown.
      p.   cm.
   ISBN 0-8007-5531-6
   1. Joy—Religious aspects—Christianity. 2. Happiness—Religious aspects—Christianity. 3. Suffering—Religious aspects—Christianity. 4. Brown, Elizabeth B. I. Title.
   BV4647.J68B76   1994
   241'.4—dc20   94-36791

Unless otherwise noted, Scripture quotations are from the HOLY BIBLE, NEW INTERNATIONAL VERSION®. NIV®. Copyright© 1973, 1978, 1984 by International Bible Society. Used by permission of Zondervan Publishing House. All rights reserved.

Scripture quotations identified KJV are from the King James Version of the Bible.

Scripture quotations identified NKJV are from The New King James Version. Copyright© 1979, 1980, 1982, Thomas Nelson, Inc., Publishers.

Dedicated to
Roy D. and **Lois P. Bowie**
who taught us when to not quit
and, importantly, how to quit

Contents

The Joy Choice

JOY COMES WHEN YOU TURN
FROM LOOKING FOR HAPPINESS
OUTSIDE YOURSELF
AND DISCOVER THE SOURCE
OF JOY IS WITHIN YOUR SPIRIT
AND IN YOUR RELATIONSHIP
TO GOD.

Key to Joy:
The door to joy is unlocked
by using God-given keys.

Our pastor, Charles Lippse, shared a great lesson he had learned as a student pastor in counseling Lester, a parishioner with serious emotional problems. Lester didn't want psychiatrists or doctors; he wanted a good spiritual man, so he sought out his church's new young pastor. In seminary, the pastoral counseling courses had emphasized nondirective counseling: Don't confront, let the one seeking counsel find his or her own solutions. So Charles faithfully heeded the advice of his professors in session after session, but Lester was not improving; if anything, he seemed worse for the wear.

One day Lester came for another hour of problem-lamenting and was hotly going on and on about the difficulties of his life as Charles, in his noncombative style, listened respectfully. Suddenly, in walked the janitor, who was a friend of Lester's. He grabbed Lester by the shirt collar as he swung the hammer in his hand wildly in the air and said, "Les, if you don't shut up and snap out of it, I'm going to split your head open with this hammer!" To Charles's amazement, Lester shook off his preoccupation, smiled, and said to him, "Joe surely knows how to talk to a fellow, don't he?!"

This book is going to talk to you! I'm not swinging a hammer, but I am crying out, "Do you want to be happy?" You can go around lamenting like Lester or you can pay attention, shake off your preoccupation, and turn your life around. Wherever you are in your life, if you aren't whistling with joy on the inside, you have become too engrossed with your problems to see the happiness within your grasp.

The Joy Choice is about finding that happiness. Happiness is an inside job—*your* job! No one can find it for you, but once you have it, no one can take joy away from you either. Sometimes life's challenges make you feel that the goal of a deep inner happiness is a dream state, but it isn't! Joy is real, tangible, obtainable, and abundant. More importantly, joy can be yours if you are willing to choose it.

I watched our youngest daughter grow in her ability to choose, to survive with joy. LeeAnne had developed child-hood-onset diabetes at the age of two. Dr. Alan Drash, America's foremost child diabetes specialist, told us diabetes was the cruelest of all childhood diseases, not because death was imminent, but because life became such a challenge. He warned us we would be engulfed by LeeAnne's disease, for her survival would depend on our fastidious care.

LeeAnne was a brittle diabetic. Her sugar levels swung sky-high and then bottomed out; they plateaued, peaked, or plummeted depending on excitement, activity, and infection. We could diagnose an oncoming viral or bacterial infection several days before she showed outward signs by her peaking sugar levels, even though her food intake and insulin remained the same. Excitement at school or home could swing her from enthusiastic and cheery to semi-comatose in a matter of minutes. Several times in the first years of her diabetes she was carried to my car by a teacher who would say, "LeeAnne has had a busy day. She fell asleep after recess. Guess she needs a good nap." Nap? She was almost unconscious. She needed food to drive her energy back up to a functioning level.

LeeAnne grew and adjusted. We learned and adjusted. Our lives changed dramatically. In our constant vigil the daytime was juggled according to Lee's activities; our night routines were adjusted to monitor her breathing. During activity it is easy to spot drops because of mood and energy swings, but at night one must listen to the deepening breathing of the diabetic. If it is too deep, action must be taken. Failure to respond to the body's needs could mean destroyed brain cells or even death.

Was LeeAnne handicapped by all this? No. She was extraordinary, wonderful, bubbly, bouncy, a loved and cherished charmer. She deserved pity and the right to whimper; instead, she brought sunlight into life. Several times every day she was forced to choose the direction of her moments. She chose to be happy.

Choosing Happiness

We watched Lee choose happiness during an afternoon of fun at Watauga Lake.

We live in the Virginia-Tennessee-North Carolina mountain-lake region, a wonderful place with great recreation areas. On a gorgeous summer day we were primed for a water-ski outing with the family. LeeAnne loved to water-ski and she was quite good for a six-year-old. We had given her an energy-filled snack in anticipation of the excitement and skiing activity. However, by the time we got the boat into the lake, had skis on Lee, and began pulling her up, she was feeling terrible. We could hear her fussing over the roar of the churning waters and the boat's motor.

Stopping the boat, we addressed the problem. "LeeAnne, we can hear your fretting all the way from back where you are up to the front of the boat. We know you must not be feeling well right now. You must make a choice: Either come into the boat until you begin to feel better or decide to enjoy where you are even though your body is not feeling well."

The choice was LeeAnne's. We could not do anything to make her feel better. We had adjusted her food intake, done everything we could do. She had a health problem and she had to deal with it. Lee sat in the water a moment, looked at us and said, "I want to ski!" As the boat pulled her out of the water, we saw a huge grin spread over her face. We could hear her singing at the top of her lungs over the motor's roar, "You are my sunshine, my only sunshine. You make me happy when skies are gray." Her little body swung in cadence to her enthusiastic song.

We had to choose happiness too. Dealing with an ailing child is traumatic. I am a teacher, not a nurse. My sense of squeamishness was challenged when I was asked to deal with a chronic health problem involving blood, needles, seizures, and medical testing. But Lee was our child and if we couldn't handle her problem, how would we help her believe that she could? Our entire family was valiantly committed to helping LeeAnne accept and cope with diabetes realistically, but *realistically* did not mean allowing her to give in to the emotions that would cry out, *You deserve pity. Stop trying. You have too much to bear to be happy.* We needed to be strong for LeeAnne's sake and for the teachers, family members, and friends who were frightened.

Everyone has a share of difficulties. This was ours and LeeAnne's. We told her everyone has problems: I wear glasses, our son Paul has an allergy to dust, some of us are less athletic than others, some of us don't do as well in school as others. No matter how large or small the problem, we have to meet the challenges we are given and trust God that he will grant us the strength to live above our difficulties.

LeeAnne became a beacon, drawing people to her like a magnet. She did not walk; she bounced. She wore a tutu to kindergarten and danced as she crossed the street to the school; then she curtsied to the cars stopped in a line by the school guard. In church she would eagerly watch the face of the minister as he gave the children's sermon, answer his questions about the God who loved her enough to make her so "perfect," and stop to kiss someone as she returned to her seat. Her soul was filled with laughter.

The Choice to Go On

LeeAnne had shown us that the choice to be happy or to wallow in self-pity is not dependent on one's age. Our family had confronted the issues of trusting God with our lives when we dealt with a sick child, knowing she faced blindness, gradual tissue and organ damage, and early death. But it was not until we confronted the ultimate test of trust, the death of LeeAnne, that we fully realized all the choices that had to be made to live beyond the circumstances of our lives.

LeeAnne died from a Reye's-type viral encephalitis one week before her seventh birthday. Her death was sudden, unexpected, devastating. We had heard of Reye's syndrome, the insidious virus that attacked like flu but within hours claimed the lives of children throughout America. Though we ached to help, we knew not to give aspirin because Lee's flu-like symptoms could become deadly when combined with acetylsalicylic acid, aspirin's base. We did not give aspirin when Lee went from lively, dancing, and laughing, to sick, lethargic, and in pain with a ter-

*Joy is broader and deeper
than positive thinking.
Joy is dependence on God,
regardless of the circumstances.*

rible headache. We cuddled her, checked with pediatricians, watched her, agonized in the hospital, and then held her as she died.

Medical teams rushed in to restart her heart, plugged her into monitors, put a screw in her skull to relieve the brain swelling. She died anyway. We went from planning her birthday party to planning her funeral service—in four days. Her death was a bomb that exploded and threatened our entire family, our beliefs, our outlook, our desire to go on living. We chose to not quit. It was the most difficult choice I have ever made! In the process of survival we learned critical lessons that may help you as you face your challenges.

We learned that joy is a choice, not a given. To live with joy is not dependent on our circumstances. Emotion-driven happiness wants life to be perfect, and then, *more* perfect. This self-centered focus is never satisfied; it constantly cries out, *I want more, I need more, I deserve more.* In contrast, joy can find peace within all circumstances. Joy allows our spirits to soar above the hurts of the past or the pain in the present. Joy grants us new eyes to see our difficulties as points of growth in life. Joy teaches us that even mountainous problems don't have to keep us down.

Joy is broader and deeper than positive thinking. Joy is more than *willing* life to be happy. You cannot *will* yourself to feel happy when your child dies, your business fails, your marriage falls apart, your health is deteriorating, or your children have major problems. Positive thinking can make one feel happy, but the more life hits, the more difficult it is to sustain happy feelings. Joy is the opposite of *self* controlling the circumstances and *self* making happiness. Joy is dependence on God, regardless of the circumstances. It comes by letting go of the controls and trusting God with your life.

Norman Vincent Peale and Robert Schuller have been maligned by many Christian groups for overemphasizing positive thinking, yet their focus on God as the source of positive thinking is truth. Positive thinking is the natural flowing from God to you as you give him your worries and concerns and allow his positive love to flood your soul. Only when people try to think positive in their own power do they fall into difficulties with positive thinking. Joy is positive thinking because we trust God can bring good from all things. "And we know that in all things God works for the good of those who love him" (Rom. 8:28).

The source of joy lies in recognizing each moment of life as a gift. Trusting that God has a purpose in *all* your life

> *Faith, not understanding,*
> *is the key to trusting.*

experiences frees you to see both joys and tragedies as opportunities for blessings. Trusting does not mean we stop striving or throw out goals. Reaching for our potential is a good use of our talents, but we must understand that merely accomplishing or attaining a goal will not make us happy. Joy is packaged in *all* of our living, not just our goal-reaching or fun-filled moments. Choosing joy in all moments of living as we move toward our objectives is the key to finding happiness along life's way.

God offers us keys to unlock the doors of a joy-filled life, keys that are not dependent on age, maturity, health, wealth, or education. Using God's keys we become dependent on his direction for our choices and gain insight into our responsibility. Faith, not understanding, is the key to trusting. Many times as the outward circumstances of our lives turn sour, we cry out, "Why?" Yet even in these times, walking with faith we can trust that God will return our swirling emotions to a sense of peace and joy.

I listened as God directed me from the catacombs of despair. I had tried so hard to deny how horribly I hurt, to

Only God can free you!

trust, to hang tight, to show courage, but as the days continued I thought I would die. Had I not felt God's voice within my inner being, I think I would have given up.

I remember the moment I let LeeAnne go. I was on an Emmaus Walk, there only to appease friends who felt it would be good for me. A year and a half had passed since Lee's death and I was not sure God deserved my being on a religious retreat. I had stayed in church, been a Sunday school teacher, kept the family going, and tried to keep my chin up, yet I was still so unhappy.

Confronted with people on the retreat who were saying how wonderful the world was, how great God was, and how blessed life was, I felt emotions swell that I had never faced. *Why did you take my little girl? Why did you let her die?* We had done battle with disease, sleeping lightly to listen to the sounds of her breathing, explaining to her teachers how to handle her drops in energy, dealing with so many physical and emotional demands, and we had won! Lee was whole, healthy, a charming child, talented, and she was ours! Surely we were not so bad as to warrant more trials. Why would God allow us to stay in such pain after her death?

In the Book of Job, we read how Job struggled to justify God's actions to his friends and himself, to try to accept fate, until finally he grew angry and began to let out the inner pain. He dropped the facade he had not even known was there as he had tried to cope and carry on in his own power. Job let go, and when he did, he had the same realization that I had. We cannot handle the pain, the loss, on our own. Only God has the strength to hold us above the drowning waters of our despair. Only God can free us so we can turn again with joy to living. Only God can free *you!*

Look at what happened when Job turned loose his hurts and put his trust in God:

> So the LORD blessed the latter end of Job more than his beginning: for he had fourteen thousand sheep, and six thousand camels, and a thousand yoke of oxen and a thousand she asses. He had also seven sons and three daughters . . . and in all the land were no women found so fair as the daughters of Job.
>
> Job 42:12–15 KJV

Job retired and lived to see his son's sons for four generations. He died, being old and full of days. He died in peace and with laughter and joy in his heart, even with the holes in his soul.

Terrible tragedy. Job made it. I made it. My husband made it. My children made it. For many, that isn't the normal scenario. You have to choose to live again, and if you fail to make the conscious decision to face the pain, life falls apart and joy runs away. Existence turns to anguish and mere survival. In *The Treatment of Families in Crisis*, Donald Langsley and David M. Kaplan detail the dangers we faced: Within two years, 75 percent of those who have lost a child are divorced. Can you picture how many are together within six years? Half of those who lose a child report serious health problems within two years—35 percent are under psychiatric care; 25 percent report psychosomatic disorders, such as ulcers, colitis, or hypertension, in a family member; 40 percent have a serious drinking or drug problem; 48 percent have at least one child with serious school problems; 43 percent report significant difficulty in the mother's homemaking ability; 88 percent feel a family member to be abnormally consumed with morbid grief reactions.[*]

Where were we in two years? We were healing, still missing LeeAnne, still with a hole in our souls, different, but moving in the direction of joy again. The battle to be happy was the toughest in my life. I fought LeeAnne's death; I fought me; I fought my past; I had to let go and forgive. I had to confront the reality of my failures and the reality of those who had failed me and let those hurts go. It took two years to release the longing for LeeAnne. It took even longer to complete the "quitting" process of the past injustices that her death brought to the surface. The loss in the present hits all the losses of life and brings them to the front.

We did more than survive the death of our child; we became conquerors, filled with joy and happiness again, but also with a greater depth of appreciation for each moment of life. Human needs want to cling to difficulties, to justify failures by them, to seek revenge. God's Spirit empowers us to live with joy beyond our circumstances; centered on self we are riddled with pity as we wallow in

---

[*]Donald Langsley and David M. Kaplan, *The Treatment of Families in Crisis* (New York: Grune, 1988).

the "whys." Trusting that there is a purpose and that good can come from all things is more difficult than following our feelings. Yet once we have tasted the freedom that trust brings, we will never want to do it alone again.

Happiness birthed by joy is an inside decision. You must fight against the human tendency to be hurt by someone else's failure to see your needs. You must become an incurable optimist, not an optimist that wears rose-colored glasses and does not see the reality of life; rather, an optimist that says, "Thanks to God I am filled with joy, a joy that transcends all of life." With him you, too, can find peace and joy, even in troubled waters.

The apostle Paul beamed his joy in the midst of travail. He learned to trust God, to feel God's Spirit working in him, interceding for him when he was too weak from troubles to carry his own weight. He learned how to be strong—he quit trying to do it on his own. He saw that

> Neither death nor life, neither angels nor demons, neither the present nor the future, nor any powers, neither height nor depth, nor anything else in all creation, will be able to separate us from the love of God that is in Christ Jesus our Lord.
>
> Romans 8:38–39

As we share the keys we learned traveling the rocky path to joy, you may find ways to confront the issues you are facing. Perhaps seeing that we did not always choose wisely will help you let go of your guilt when you fail. Study with us as we look at the lives of those faithful to God in the Bible, those who, like us, made good and bad decisions, but ultimately learned to trust God. You, too, can learn to live above the circumstances of your life with joy, even in the midst of the difficulties. *The Joy Choice* will share with you the keys to becoming free, free to be what God has intended you to be.

Do you want that freedom? Are you bearing difficulties and hurts that overwhelm you? Follow us and see how we grew to trust. You, too, can thrill in every moment of life, even the difficult moments. You can live with a bad marriage and be happy—perhaps even bring about a good marriage through your changed attitude. Your changing has the potential to change others, though it may not do so. You may not be able to change a dysfunctional family, but you can quit being dysfunctional. Your bad past need not destroy the potential for a good present. Your life can change for the better as you learn to choose joy.

Take hold of God's keys. He will direct you quietly. He will force you to confront your hurts, and though it will be painful, you must face yourself in order to heal. Seeing who you are can be the toughest part of the whole process. Recognizing that God already knows who you *are*, not just who you pretend to be, and still loves you can give you the courage to break the bonds that keep you tied.

Come with us as we work our way toward freedom. Choosing joy is more than an attitude change. It is a dynamic process that will change your life. I can't wait to share God's diamonds with you!

Questions

1. How does age, sex, wealth, or education affect our ability to find joy?
2. What is the source of radiating inner joy?
3. Give some basic differences between joy and happiness. Can you think of others?
4. How can you tell whether a positive attitude is flowing from God or is self-directed?
5. Describe the growth process of someone in the Bible toward a joy-filled life.
6. Describe the difficulties a Bible character brought into his life and the life of his family as he searched for happiness.

7. Have you, or has someone in your life, found joy?
    How do you know? Describe your/their journey to
    joy.

Diamonds

◊ *The choice to be happy or to wallow in self-pity
  is not dependent on one's age, health, sex, wealth,
  or education.*

◊ *Joy is dependent on "I" changing to "with God."*

◊ *Joy is a* choice, *not a given.*

◊ *Choosing joy is a dynamic process.*

◊ *Trusting God is the secret to joy, not everything
  in life going our way.*

◊ *Unhappy emotions are overcome gradually.*

◊ *Joy is positive thinking that flows from a close
  walk with God.*

moments when your pain threshold tolerates only so much before it screams, *Whoa! Too much!* Most of our difficulties are played out on this plane where suffering of any degree merges into one thought, *I hurt.*

The way in which we accept our life challenges and all the suffering they entail can determine whether they will give us the opportunity to grow. We either will remain brave, unselfish, and caring, or we will become immersed in self-concern. You may be suffering hurts in relationships, losses, low self-esteem, or numerous other challenges. To move on, you must communicate your needs to God so he can give you the courage to meet your challenges.

Communicating with God

A child communicates by reaching for his daddy's hands or face. Reaching for his father's hands is a search for something, a "gimme." Reaching for his father's face is a gesture of love, "I love you, Daddy." God wants us to seek his face. He longs for us to communicate with him in the trusting, adoring, and love-filled manner of a small child reaching to touch his daddy tenderly. To find joy you must communicate with God hand-to-face.

Talking *to* God is often easier than talking *with* God. When LeeAnne developed diabetes I was devastated. I did not know how to communicate my distress to God. God knew I did not want my child to have a disease that would limit her life. My prayers were simple, "God, thank you for my little girl. Help me to help her deal with this great health problem." I was talking *to* God, not *with* him. My hands were reaching for his hands, not his face.

I should have shared with God how I was hurting because my child was struggling up a mountain. Communicating with God when we hurt can be our biggest hurdle because we confuse trust with resignation. We build walls as we try to hold up on our own. LeeAnne's health

*Communication through prayer
brings release from trying to
handle life alone, builds trust, and
opens our lives to God's grace.*

situation might not have changed had I shared my deep-
est emotions, but my feelings about it could have, if I had
communicated with him hand-to-face. My feeling that I had
to shoulder the load on my own because God had allowed
the disease could have been transformed to a knowledge
that God would bring good from the difficulty. LeeAnne's
death finally brought me to a communication level with
God. Crying out of my hurt, no longer able to justify or hold
it together on my own, I reached in pain for his face as I
cried out, "Why couldn't you have let us keep LeeAnne?"

The parallel between our human relationships and our
spiritual relationship is the same: We must communicate
to have closeness and understanding. Communication
opens the door to trust. Denying that we hurt keeps self-
control in the driver's seat and our relationship with God
on the "gimme" level; sharing our hurt with God allows
him to wrap us in his arms, giving us the strength to endure
or to let go. Sharing lets us know God cares, as his grace
flows from his face through our fingertips to fill even our
difficult moments with a sense of abiding joy.

Many times we turn prayer into a one-way conversa-
tion. "Dear God, *I* need. Dear God, *I* want. Dear God, *I*
hurt." Prayer that works in a two-way path takes away the
stress on "I." It involves talking, listening, and waiting for
God's grace. Hand-to-face communication brings God's

grace to the underpinnings of your life as it unfolds a double power: *release* from trying to handle life alone and the *outpouring* of God's love to undergird you.

God's grace fills us and frees us from the crippling stabs of "I need," changing our attitude to "thank you." Your problems may not change, but your need to control the situation changes. I could not reverse LeeAnne's health, but with God's help I could trust him to give us the grace to handle our emotional needs. Talking *with* him, rather than *at* him, allowed me to feel his underpinning support.

Grace, God's Love Flowing within Us

Grace cleanses our lives. As God's love calls us to him, he wipes away the dust and begins filling our hearts with love. The balloon of our spirit begins to fill with clean air as the dust clears, until finally we are freed from the weight of our difficulties, failures, and bondages. In *Mere Christianity*, C. S. Lewis describes grace as God injecting his kind of life and thought into a tin soldier, turning the dead, staid, confined piece of metal into a live man. Grace changes you. The process takes time. Grace brings change that slowly fills your life with joy. God's life-changing grace:

- Gives courage
- Energizes us for our task
- Frees us
- Brings love-filled change
- Releases and affirms
- Helps us value the individual
- Supports and encourages
- Fills us with joy

Grace empowers us to love our world as God opens our eyes to the value of all people and gives us the love to support and encourage their growth. We are freed to love even the difficult people in our lives. As grace frees us to love others, it also gives us the assurance that God loves us. We can have confidence that even in the dark times of life, we are safe in God's love and able, at any time, to reach toward his face.

Choosing Hand-to-Face Communication

Because Christ in his human nature suffered and was tempted in all points as we are, he struggled to give the controls of his life over to God, just as you and I do. Faced with the knowledge of his own execution, his turbulent

---

*Peace flows through submission,
not resignation.*

---

thoughts argued against the unfairness. His emotional plea to God in the Garden of Gethsemane was so urgent and physically exhausting that sweat from his brow was like drops of blood. He shared everything with God—his fears, disappointments, and chaotic emotions—so God's grace could empower him to handle life . . . and death.

Christ needed the support of others, just as you and I do, so he was saddened by his sleeping disciples who did not recognize the seriousness of his plight. Did they not care enough about his struggle to stay awake and pray? He felt alone. His anticipated sacrifice felt too costly. Surely God could change the plan so that the travail of crucifixion would be unnecessary. Christ pleaded.

We, too, pleaded when faced with LeeAnne's death. Faith was there; the petition was there; God's caring was there. But we had to let go of our own human desires. You have to let go of handling life in your own strength, too. How grateful I am that Christ can be our advocate because he has personal experience with the emotions that threaten our sense of peace and trust in times of travail. Christ showed us that in the difficult times in our lives, it is not the standing tall that brings peace to our hearts. Peace comes as we kneel in prayer to communicate our hurts and needs. Through grace we are empowered with courage to carry on. Peace flows through submission, not resignation.

Choice is the difference between being a victor or being a victim. We choose whether we will communicate with God to overcome our struggles or build walls and form a monument to our own suffering. No one is without choice. We had to *decide* to move on. You must choose too. The shock we experienced immediately after LeeAnne's death is a healthy, short-term, temporary coping technique in extreme conditions. But even though most of life takes place in milder climates, we must continue to adjust, change, and grow.

Choosing to trust when confronted with life requires direct communication with God, even as our emotions rage. As you are being hit by life's storms, remember that Christ talked to God about his life's path *before* he moved to acceptance. If Christ, who had perfect communion with God, went to God to appeal, we must do the same. Christ showed us that in the difficult times of our lives, it is not the standing tall that brings peace to our hearts; it is the kneeling in prayer as we communicate our hurts and needs. Peace can only flow through submission, not resignation. God was never more human than in the Garden of Gethsemane. He is never nearer to us than when we hurt. Pay attention. The hand that reaches out to you when you cry out your needs may be a pierced one.

Questions

1. Why is prayer necessary when God already knows our needs?
2. How does prayer make the impossible possible?
3. What is the force released by two-way communication with God?
4. How does God's grace empower you?
5. What is the difference between seeking God's hands and seeking God's face?
6. Does God understand your battle with faith and struggle in life's challenges? Justify your answer.

Diamonds

◊ *You can choose your response to any of life's challenges, with God's help.*
◊ *No one is without choice.*
◊ *Prayer gives us the grace to handle our course.*
◊ *Choice is the difference between being a victor or being a victim.*
◊ *Joy requires hand-to-face communication.*
◊ *Grace takes time to feel, gives courage, energizes, frees, brings love-filled change, and fills us with joy.*
◊ *Kneeling, not standing tall, is the act that brings grace.*

Happiness
Is an
Inside Job

3

WHAT YOU THINK
IS WHAT YOU ARE!

Key to Joy:
Healthy love strengthens your character
as it builds your ego.

Anyone who has struggled to rid a lawn of weeds appreciates their tenacity and perseverance. Cut the grass short and the dandelions will stay short and flat, with flowers just below the height of the mower blades and leaves just high enough to choke out nearby grass. Let your grass grow tall and the dandelions will grow tall. Pull them out and even the smallest root will grow another plant. Use weed killer and the dandelion will die, leaving a barren place to become a perfect seedbed for new dandelions.

Thoughts, like weeds, can grow out of control, bringing pesky problems into your life. Thoughts that build your ego without strengthening your character will cause your "inside lawn" to spring up in dandelion-like, pesky, out-of-control problems that threaten happiness. Weeds that creep into your character can destroy you, damage your relationships, and rid your life of joy.

The wisdom that keeps thoughts in line is not an automatic process that matures with years. Nothing comes with

---

Thoughts are the seedbed of actions.

---

age, except wrinkles. Healthy thoughts grow healthy as they are centered in God's principles and maintained by God's guidance. But even though we may know how to have positive, strengthening thoughts, we still allow weeds to creep into our character. We allow our mind's thoughts to direct our body's actions!

Christ knew that thoughts are the seedbed of our actions. What we think, we will become; that is why Scripture stresses positive thinking, centered in God.

> Whatever is true, whatever is noble, whatever is right, whatever is pure, whatever is lovely, whatever is admirable —if anything is excellent or praiseworthy—think about such things.
>
> Philippians 4:8

God-centered thoughts bring abundant, joy-filled life as their end product.

Character and Thoughts— the Hand and Glove of the Mind

The relationship between our character and our thoughts is like that of a hand and a glove. Though separate, they are very much the same—what one does the other does, what one encourages the other joins, what one becomes affects the other. Character produces a pattern of behavior that is acted out through personality and moral standards. Character affects the thoughts that drive our behavior and personality. On the other hand, our thoughts stimulate, direct, and even change our character by re-directing our actions.

Character	Thoughts
• Affects thoughts	• Affect character
• Drives behavior	• Stimulate behavior
• Directs personality	• Affect personality
• Patterns our value system	• Sway moral behavior

No one in history has understood the relationship be-tween our thoughts and our character as Christ did. His understanding of our spiritual nature and the nature of God bring us incredible and revolutionary insights. Christ repeatedly stressed the relationship of our thoughts to our actions. He did so in the Sermon on the Mount.

> You have heard that it was said to the people long ago, "Do not murder," and anyone who murders will be subject to judgment. But I tell you that anyone who is angry with his brother will be subject to judgment.... You have heard that it was said, "Do not commit adultery." But I tell you that anyone who looks at a woman lustfully has already com-mitted adultery with her in his heart.
>
> Matthew 5:21–22, 27–28

We survived the first few days after our child's death by controlling our thoughts. We focused on how many ways people had blessed LeeAnne's life and how blessed our family had been to have had such a precious child. Deter-mined to celebrate LeeAnne's life in the funeral service, we changed the order of worship into a service of cele-bration. The half hour prior to the service, Jane LaPella, our dedicated church organist, played light, bubbly music on the piano. The songs rang with cheer, childish laugh-ter, and love of life. Instead of a sermon, Reverend Ernest

Cushman made a few remarks about the value of life, especially a young life, then gave the invitation for members of the congregation to share a favorite memory of LeeAnne. Anecdotes came from throughout the congregation and memories were shared of the way LeeAnne had touched lives. No one left the service without realizing the value and intertwining of our lives with one another.

The loss of LeeAnne, such an important part of our lives, was devastating. Dwelling on something positive was our lifeline to sanity in the midst of horror. The days, months,

---

Joy is a choice to think of life as a blessing.

---

and years following the service, we still fought our emotions in order to dwell on the blessings LeeAnne had brought into our lives, as opposed to the devastating hole we were experiencing without her. Staying focused on the positive, forcing ourselves to think of the blessings when our souls cried out in loss, was the key to our healthy survival and eventual healing.

Thoughts *do* control our actions. Insidiously they begin to direct our paths. Positive thoughts pulled us through each day and kept us moving toward the goal of peace within our circumstances. Negative thoughts could have pulled us under. When *Sunrise Tomorrow* was published, I was invited by Jeannie Crumley to autograph books at Zimmerman's Bookstore in Johnson City. The event was special, a positive blessing spawned by a great loss, a time to share, a rare moment of life.

The most poignant moment of the afternoon, however,

was not positive. A fifty-year-old mother who had lost her son thirty years before asked me to autograph a book for her. She moaned and lamented as she shared in detail the loss of her son and her subsequent grief-filled life. The loss of her son was tragic; her choice to continue to dwell on

Unhealthy thoughts come in through logical doors.

the loss was a double tragedy. She had destroyed her life by the thoughts she chose. I left depressed by the thought that maybe I would never be able to live with joy if that mother had been unable to find happiness after thirty years. My choice to find joy, however, had begun the moment LeeAnne died, as I began to focus on the blessing her life had been to me as opposed to the loss.

Fortunately, even if we had focused on the loss as the woman in the bookstore did, at any point in time we could have turned ourselves around, said, "Move on," and started to think of our blessings again. Time, age, sex, maturity, difficulty, strength—all of these are factors, but none are the reason we live joyously. Joy indwells as we choose to think of life as a blessing in the midst of the good, the challenging, and the tragic.

Holes in Our Character

Choosing actions and thoughts that build character is not easy, for unhealthy thoughts come in through logical doors. Holes in our character are caused as we justify what we want to do when we know it is not what we should do.

We are never tempted to do wrong by things that seem unreasonable. The first instinct against wrong is rejection, but if it is nursed in the mind long enough, the mind begins to find ways to rationalize that it is acceptable. Christ said that it is not only adultery that is evil, but lustful thoughts as well, because he knew that mind games can influence character and allow an evil seed to grow into a wrong action.

King David is a solid example of the way thoughts begin to warp character. No one in the Hebrew nation had a stronger sense of right and wrong than David did as a young man. People respected his ability to stand up for right in the midst of danger, threats, injustice, and persecution. As a young man David was firmly planted in God's will. David never meant to close God out. He certainly did not recognize he was moving away from God's direction for an abundant life.

I empathize with David. The mighty king of Israel, charming, handsome, rich, beloved by his people, had everything... but a good marriage. Confronted with problems on every front in his career, home needed to be a retreat and a comfort. Instead, it was part of the battleground. Friction reigned in his home. The following passage demonstrates what home life was like for David after the greatest military triumph of his career.

> As the ark of the LORD was entering the City of David, Michal daughter of Saul watched from a window. And when she saw King David leaping and dancing before the LORD, she despised him in her heart. . . .
>
> When David returned home to bless his household, Michal daughter of Saul came out to meet him and said, "How the king of Israel has distinguished himself today, disrobing in the sight of the slave girls of his servants as any vulgar fellow would!"
>
> David said to Michal, "It was before the LORD, who chose me rather than your father or anyone from his house when

1. Do everything for positive reasons. Fulfill obligations because you feel good about sharing your time and abilities, not because someone will be irritated with you if you don't. Be positive about your role. Doing things for positive reasons creates positive responses in your life.

2. Let yourself cry—and laugh! Don't be afraid of your emotions. Express yourself. On the other hand, don't become lost in your emotions. Tricky balance, but well worth the effort. Laughter brings lightness and joy to the heart. Throw back your head and laugh uproariously. Laughter feels good!

3. Celebrate. You don't have to have big occasions to celebrate. Celebrate your child's first six weeks in school, your dog's loyalty, a friendship, a finished project. Did you finally clean up the yard? Do something special. If you make a habit of celebrating even the small events, your life takes on greater significance and you begin seeing blessings in the everyday moments of life.

4. Be a memory maker. Find ways to build memories. Good memories are built from someone taking time to remind you that you are special to them. It may be fun and games, like stringing a room with twine from light to bed, up, down, and around, or a significant special occasion like a Sweet Sixteen party. Memories are what hold families together, build joy in aloneness, make the moments together more special.

5. Give thanks. Tell someone how special he or she is! Start looking for occasions to thank the people in your life for the things they do to make your world better—your child, the teacher, a janitor, store clerk, plumber, or parent. Write a letter telling someone what he or she means to you. Pick up the phone and call to say, "Thank you."

6. Hug yourself. Fall asleep reading one of your favorite books. Read until you can no longer keep your eyes open. Enjoy the pleasure of doing something you love to do, just because you want to. Knowing you have done something with no particular value except pure enjoyment brings a renewed vigor. You don't have to be productive to find pleasant feelings.

7. *Take a long bath or shower.* Luxuriate. Use bath oils, fragrances. Warm the towels. Wrap up in a big robe and do nothing for ten whole minutes.

8. *Exercise.* The mind doesn't work well when the body is sluggish. A balanced life requires a balanced mind and body. Exercise, rest, and work are a crucial team. When life seems the most hectic, take fifteen minutes to do some form of exercise. All systems will work more efficiently when exercise perks them up.

9. *Plan for something special.* Plan a trip, a party, an outing, a visit—whatever! Planning and dreaming keep joy alive.

10. *Immerse yourself in Scripture and pray.* Take time to be with God. Having a strong base of Scripture gives guidance and strength. Insights into human and spiritual nature flow when you are attentive to God's Word.

Questions

1. King David is a solid example of the way thoughts can warp character. Explain.
2. What is the difference between proactive and reactive thoughts? How do they affect your character and ego?
3. How can bad thoughts corrupt good character?
4. Give some techniques to keep thoughts healthy as we handle emotions, challenges, responsibilities, and commitments.
5. What does it mean when we say, "You are a product of your thoughts"?
6. What is the key to healthy thoughts that will build our ego and character?

7. How are wrong thoughts in our minds like dandelions in a lawn?

Diamonds

◊ *Right thoughts are God-directed through quiet
  guidance and the concrete rules and principles
  found in Scripture.*

◊ *Thoughts can be redirected at any time, before,
  during, or after we find ourselves caught by
  immoral, negative, or wrong actions.*

◊ *Thoughts are the seedbed of actions.*

◊ *Rejection is the first instinct against wrong, but
  nurse the wrong long enough and the mind will
  rationalize the rightness of even the most vile
  action.*

◊ *Proactive we impact the world; reactive we react
  to life as it hits us.*

When the Unexpected Happens

4

YOU WILL EITHER FOCUS ON
THE POSSIBILITIES
OR BE CONSUMED BY THE
IMPOSSIBILITIES.

Key to Joy:
Safely flying out of the nest
depends on where you center your focus.

J watched a mother bird teach her two chicks to fly today. As I watched her land, I saw a nest balanced on a wooden beam in our garage with two baby birds perched expectantly on its rim. The mother would fly and the babies would flap; then, chickening out, they would twitter, shiver, and shake. She would return, chirp encouragement, flap around, and then fly again. I could feel the baby birds' trepidation and the reassuring urging of the mother, *Come on. You can do it. Don't be afraid. Watch me. Try.*

The laborious encouragement took thirty minutes before the first chick flapped off the nest edge and flew. She was not very good and didn't go very far, but, she flew and flapped enough to land halfway calculated on the soft grass near the concrete. That left the tinier bird alone, shaking with fear, knowing he needed to go but so afraid he wanted to hide. *Off went sister with mother. Maybe they will never return.* He looked out, peeped, shook, and flapped. He fell back into the nest, then jumped to the edge again and screamed, *Where's my mother?*

The mother was sheltering the first chick. Hidden in a bush, the courageous chick's chest was heaving. Jumping off a nest into thin air is no easy task, even for a bird. The mother flew back to the tiny chick, who, by this time, was in a state of panic. No way was he going to jump off that nest. The mother chirped and flew off. *Come back! Don't leave me. I can't! Why are you doing this? I don't want to fly.*

The mother took her chicks on flying lessons for an hour or more. Neither would flutter more than a few feet at first. Flutter, lift, nosedive, flutter, flutter, wing dive, flutter, flutter, fly. What a precious memory. I was uplifted, the chicks were exhausted, and the mother looked worn out but was chirping.

God must have been elated when he saw me fly. I had not wanted to leave my nest. I couldn't believe what was happening and wanted to rest in my safe little abode. Fly? No way! I saw the concrete below, and, good grief, I was barely handling the nest's rim. The time of my flight was most unexpected, as are most real flying lessons. Come with me to a time when my family gathered to celebrate and instead took a lesson in flying that would change our perspective on trust forever.

Confronting the Unexpected

After LeeAnne died, I watched my father live through four torturous years of multiple myeloma cancer. He did not give up during the four years of hospitalization, treatment, medicines, and destruction. He lost his stamina, his muscle strength, his health. His spine collapsed five inches, threatening to sever nerves. X rays showed his bones to look like Swiss cheese where the cancer had formed its bone-dissolving tumors. He had every right to suffer outrage, to scream at the injustices, to quit. Yet he chose to survive and to be happy, chipper, and optimistic. He was

absolutely victorious, even though the eventual outcome
of his disease process was death.

The colossal task of his survival took tremendous courage. Regaining strength when the radiation treatments, sur-
geries, and medicines destroyed cells was a struggle. He
fought for the right to each moment of additional time. The
payoff was four years of life, touching others in ways normal living never affords; four years of teaching through
actions the victory the Spirit has over any foe; four years of
unquenchable joy above the cesspool of pain and struggle.
He had a problem, but the problem did not have him.

The past four years had been difficult for all of us, watching as my father became progressively weakened by the
powerful cancer. His life was down to precious weeks, each
day an additional gift of time. Our family needed reasons
to celebrate joyous occasions. So celebrating four birth-
days—my nieces Jodi and Lyndsey, my sister Amy and
me—was a welcome excuse to get together.

The morning of our celebration the phone rang. No
hello. No greeting. No cheery lilt in the voice. A nurse in
my sister Amy's obstetrics office quietly urged, "Betty,
could you come quickly? Your sister's baby has died in her
womb and she needs you." I could barely gasp. "Died?
What do you mean?" I listened numbly as she said that
Amy's obstetrician wouldn't deliver the baby until tomorrow. The doctor realized the crucial need for the family to
have worked through many of the needs and the reality
together before the birth.

My mind pirouetted to four years before when the doctors had pronounced our LeeAnne dead. The casket, the
outfit, the visitation, the service details . . . not again. A
longed-for baby, awaited by her sisters, her dad and mom,
a ray of sunshine in the darkness of my father's medical
crisis. My wings began to flutter but my heart wanted to
drop back into the nest. No way I wanted to fly. Surely this

couldn't be happening . . . but it was, and I was needed. The sadness of talking to my little nieces about the death of their sister paled in comparison to the emotional upheaval of helping Doug and Amy pick out a casket and suggesting ideas for the services. Painful memories came

*When our focus changes
to thanksgiving,
we have the ability to soar above
the surrounding circumstances.*

back to the present until I felt a staggering weight that wanted to force my body into paralysis. *No,* I told myself. *I've done this before and they need my help. Nobody gets through this kind of crisis alone.*

The day had been heaped with extreme emotion and overwhelming sadness, and now our families gathered for the birthday dinner. Quietness was draped over everyone's soul. My dad, who had been a tall, strong, virile man, was now barely able to get out of his chair. Mother was uncharacteristically silent. Doug and Amy were sheltering their children as they struggled to keep from exploding into fragments. Were we really going to sing "Happy Birthday" and open gifts?

Dad rose slowly. "Let's hold hands. I want to share a thought." God was watching us, as Dad, like the mother bird, began to lead us from the nest. "We're all hurting. We hurt for Doug and Amy, for the lost opportunity to know this little child who had already become part of our hearts. We are all struggling, needing God's arms to hold us through this tragedy. Tonight we are here to surround each other in a time of need. But we are also here to celebrate. Today is Amy's birthday. She has been granted another moment of life. It is also Jodi's, Lyndsey's, and Betty's birthday. They have been given the most precious gift of all—time. We want to thank God for the incalculable opportunities another year will bring, even as we acknowledge our pain."

My flight began. Dad did not deny that our emotions were screaming at the unexpected and unwanted change, but he helped us to refocus on the big picture of life. Life is the gift—a moment, a year, or many years. When our focus changes to thanksgiving, the key that unlocks joy, we have the ability to soar above the surrounding circumstances.

Joy's key is the focus I choose:
I choose to look at the concrete below
or I choose to fly.

The fear of that first push is lost in the wonder of flight. Like the baby birds, in all of our life's flights, we either focus on the possibilities or are consumed by the difficulties.

When the unexpected happens, it is hard to focus on thanksgiving. Deep emotions cry out for our attention. See if you recognize these reactions when change has come your way.

- Stunned, you become disorganized, disbelieving, and numb.
- Emotions escalate your anxiety and fears.

- You question life, your purpose, and God's purpose.
- You choose to move on or you stay stuck in negative emotions.

I gleaned one great insight while watching the baby birds and then later flying myself from the nest's rim: I learned the key to joy in all circumstances has nothing to do with the outside particulars. Joy's key is the focus I choose: I *choose* to look at the concrete below or I *choose* to fly. I saw the fear of the little birds change to excitement and joy as they struggled through their beginning lessons and finally flew from the nest. I felt that same courage and strength fill my spirit when my focus changed from the crisis at hand to the wonder of the life God had granted me. I realized *change is possible.* Change to a positive outlook, like flight, depends on where you focus your sight. You can change, turning negatives into positives, if you focus on the Teacher, not the concrete.

The birthday celebration brought us to an acute awareness that each time the unexpected happens, we can find ourselves right back on the edge of the nest, wondering whether we are headed for the concrete or the grass. Each time we fly from the nest, it becomes a bit easier. We begin to recognize God's grace that pulls us to peace amidst the winds of change. Yet unexpected change always catches us off guard; that is why it is crucial to trust the One giving us flying lessons!

Perhaps you have been hit by the unexpected and are on the nest's rim crying out, "Life isn't worth it!" Such thoughts are your emotions controlling your attitude. Life *is* worth the struggle. I did not think I could live through the pain, and you may be thinking the same thing. You can. You must travel a God-given route of emotional healing when the unexpected happens. As you travel, you will find your strength coming back and your wings beginning to flap.

Change's Challenge

How do we successfully handle change? Through the example of the disciples, we find these principles for dealing with unexpected change:

- Get quiet
- Listen for guidance
- Center your focus on trust
- Fly

As we look at three disciples who should have been most aware of the treasure they possessed in walking with Christ, it might be uplifting to know that even they were taken aback when they were hit by the unexpected.

> After six days Jesus took Peter, James and John with him and led them up a high mountain, where they were all alone. There he was transfigured before them. His clothes became dazzling white, whiter than anyone in the world could bleach them. And there appeared before them Elijah and Moses, who were talking with Jesus.
>
> Peter said to Jesus, "Rabbi, it is good for us to be here. Let us put up three shelters—one for you, one for Moses and one for Elijah." (He did not know what to say, they were so frightened.)
>
> Then a cloud appeared and enveloped them, and a voice came from the cloud: "This is my Son, whom I love. Listen to him!"
>
> Suddenly, when they looked around, they no longer saw anyone with them except Jesus.
>
> Mark 9:2–8

The disciples responded to unexpected change in the same way we do; they were initially stunned by the unearthly appearance of Christ emanating light from his countenance and aglow in garments so white they shone.

In times of change,
God simply wants us on our knees.

Moses and Elijah, two of the greatest spiritual heroes in Hebrew history, were conversing with Christ. Like the disciples, our first reaction to change is to become quiet as we are startled by the change confronting us. Even positive change creates momentary disbelief. Then as we perceive something unexpected is happening, our fears grow, even in the midst of the unexpected happenings that are good. What will this mean . . . new expectations, relationships, goals? We question what we should do to take control of the situation. At this point, we should continue being quiet, but escalating emotions create the "do" danger.

At first Peter, James, and John became quiet; then they began to *do*. Remember this was an exciting unexpected moment. (Imagine the "do" danger if it had been a threatening unexpected moment!) As the emotions soared, Peter said, "Let us put up three shelters" (v. 5). The Bible says that Peter spoke up with a "do" because he was afraid (v. 6). He felt so privileged. What could he do in response? Good unexpected change brings the same reaction as bad unexpected change. We fear, anxiously anticipate, or want to repay until we *do* something; then we feel we have responded properly. The simple, proper response God demands is that we fall on our knees and listen for guidance.

God surrounded the disciples with a cloud and stopped their doing (v. 7). In times of change we must keep our focus centered on trust. Soaring emotions make trust difficult, if not impossible, unless we slowly center our minds on Christ. Like the little birds learning to fly, if we stay centered on the mother bird, flight seems possible. But if we focus on the concrete, the distance to the grass, the height of the nest, or any of a million other distractions, we become overwhelmed by fears.

It is important for us to recognize that we, like the disciples, have the potential of pulling our eyes off of Christ, making it difficult to trust. Children, marriage, wealth, goals, work, difficulties, tragedies—whatever keeps you too busy to seek Christ will have the same effect on you that Elijah and Moses had on the disciples. They became frightened and in their rush to do something, they almost missed the true meaning of the moment. When the disciples recentered on Christ after God's cloud had surrounded them, they no longer saw anyone except Christ. Centering on Christ frees us from all the other distractions and allows us to trust and be still.

Being still is one of life's most difficult tasks, especially when the unexpected comes. We all want to *do* something, just as Peter, James, and John did. God requires that we seek him before we do anything and allow him to fill our spirits with his instructions. If we fail, we must get back out of the nest and try again. Get quiet, pray so that you stay centered, and then be prepared for flight. The rim of the nest is scary but force yourself to recenter on Christ. Don't be afraid as you look around. Focus your eyes on God, flap, flutter, and then fly. The impossibilities will change to possibilities.

Questions

1. What are the four reactions that take control when we are faced with unexpected change?
2. What is the "do" danger we face in response to change? Explain how the disciples responded to the unexpected as they waited for Christ.

3. What four steps must be taken to handle the unexpected wisely?
4. You successfully handled a major change in life. What will happen when unexpected change hits again?
5. Share the process of growth in trust you have seen in someone in your life.
6. What are the distractions that are keeping you from seeking Christ and resting in his trust?
7. Share a Bible story that shows someone flying from the nest. Was his or her flight a success or a failure? Why?

Diamonds

◊ *Joy depends on where we focus.*

◊ *Prayer changes our focus as it centers us.*

◊ *We either will focus on the possibilities or be consumed by the impossibilities.*

◊ *Falling on our knees is the response God wants when we experience change.*

◊ *Change, like flight, depends on where you focus your sight.*

5
Breaking Down Walls

GOD ALWAYS REACHES DOWN
TO BRING HIS PEOPLE BACK,
EVEN AS THEY BUILD WALLS
AGAINST HIM.

Key to Joy:
Faith must be alive and vital
for you to be joy-filled.

J was blessed with the heritage of a strong Christian family. I grew up knowing and trusting God with my life. Yet LeeAnne's death was so devastating that without even consciously knowing it, I built a wall to lock God out. It didn't happen right away. At first I couldn't have survived without his help. I prayed. I talked. I studied the Scriptures and listened to Christian scholars. I felt his undergirding. I knew he was holding me together, but as my hurt grew and the pain did not stop and the longing swelled, I began to struggle with who would have the control of my life— God or me.

I did not lock him out all at once. The process was slow. On the surface, I was holding up incredibly: I was alive, smiling, talking, giving lectures, writing a book, going to church, teaching, taking care of my children, loving my husband, giving birthday parties. I was trying to listen for God. But behind the scenes of my body's actions I was thinking: *Why am I still hurting? Where is God's healing? What good is*

> *God never leaves us,*
> *but we can leave him.*

---

faith anyway? I didn't recognize how empty I was until two years later when I finally talked with God. He had never left me; I had walled him out. When I opened the door and let him back in, I realized the utter emptiness I had been feeling had come from trying to handle life on my own.

I had not meant to do something that would cause more problems. I was simply trying to live after I buried my little girl. I started out in good faith, resolved to hold up and carry out my job, analyzing what would help my family make it through the storm, hanging on with each new slam of emotions. But on my own, I was in a mess!

Biblical Perspective

Throughout the Bible, there are stories of men and women who built walls and struggled to give God the controls of their lives. The wall building began in the Garden of Eden.

Adam and Eve

God walked, talked, and communed directly with the first man and woman, Adam and Eve, into whom he breathed spiritual insight and understanding. They understood God was the one true God, the Creator of all life, the Source of all authority. Yet even with God's Spirit to guide them, to walk with them, to lead them, they desired more—the controls. They felt they could live life in their own power, and thought, perhaps, they could even do it better than God. Never having been without God, they were willing to risk their closeness with him by doing what they *felt*, as opposed to what God *said* was best.

Adam and Eve did not comprehend the significance of their action, any more than I realized that the nagging little thoughts in my head were building a wall to hide me from God. Before Adam and Eve took the bite from the fruit, they had already built a wall to keep God away. God did not leave them and he did not leave me. We were the ones who walled him out as we slowly and subconsciously decided we could handle life better on our own.

The Israelites

The Israelites were God's chosen people, yet, like Adam and Eve, they were unwilling to relinquish life's controls and trust God's lead. Their faith in a personal God with whom they had a relationship was unique in that period of history when most people were worshipping stones, the sun, or mythical heroes. Relying on their emotions, just as we often do, they slowly tuned God out as they determined to make life better on their own. In order to call them back, God sent prophets to teach his love, performed miracles to show his power, and even sent angels to serve his children. For short spans of time the Israelites would listen and follow, but slowly they would abandon trust and begin to doubt again.

Change is difficult and it brought anger and fear to a peak as the Israelites struggled to move from city life to a nomadic desert existence. They moaned and longed for the days of being cared for by the Egyptians. Ten different times on the plains of the Sinai the Israelites rose against God. The blocks of their wall to keep God out were firmly in place.

Philip Yancey in *Disappointment with God* theorizes that for the Hebrews written and spoken commands with crystal-clear directions may have served the purpose of getting the mass of freed slaves across a wilderness, sea, and desert, but it did not encourage spiritual development. In fact, for the Israelites it nearly eliminated the need for faith at all. Clear guidance sucked away freedom, making every choice a matter of obedience rather than faith.

I believe the problem for the Israelites was the basic struggle for all of humanity: We like to do things our own way. We do not want to bow to authority outside ourselves. Even if life were all rosy and cheery, we would still struggle between self and God. Miracles, signs, clouds, and manna might bring security for a little while, but then life begins to hit below the belt, the questions begin to rise, and the wall begins to build.

Samson

As a young man, Samson was firmly planted in faith. But like so many before him, he allowed his selfish desires, bitterness, and need for revenge to build a wall between him and God.

The difference between doing it on your own and doing it with God is a sense of joy.

Samson was both popular and famous. He was not evil; he had lost the proper alignment of his priorities and he was caught. He had built his wall and then became encased by his desires. The Philistines, enemies of the Hebrews, knew Samson's weaknesses—women and gambling—and played on them to capture, blind, and enslave him.

Leaving God is subtle.
It happens one stone at a time.

Samson never meant to wall God out, but when his life fell apart, he should have seen the wall. Instead Samson refused to accept responsibility for the broken relationship with God. He saw only the problems brought into his life by others. Chained to a heavy millstone to grind grain in the Philistine prison, he seethed and sought revenge against the Philistines.

Samson got his wish when he pulled the temple pillars down, killing several thousand Philistines in the process. The Philistines were devastated as their leadership died in the carnage. Samson was used by God to relieve the oppression of the Hebrews, but because of the walls he had built, he was not used as God would have chosen.

With priorities centered in God, Samson's life could have been filled with peace instead of revenge and anger. Submitting to God's will means we must stop trying to do things in our own power. It means that when the storms hit or desires pull, we must submit to a greater authority. You can feel the difference between handling life alone and handling it with God. Never again do I want to erect a wall and prohibit God's working within my life.

Symptoms of Spiritual Disease and Wall Building

I did not know I was moving away from God after LeeAnne's death. I wish someone had told me there were symptoms of spiritual disease and wall building. Maybe it will help you to look at the signs and symptoms with me.

Leaving God is subtle. Age, a history of strong faith, wealth, education—none of these keeps you safe from the temptation to assert your own desire ahead of your understanding of what God wants for your life. That is crucial to remember when you have children in your care. Children can turn injustice, unfairness, hurts, and wants into anger stones as easily as adults can. Or perhaps you are older and you think your faith walk is secure because you've been walking with God a long time. Not true.

Wall building is quiet, easy to justify, very specific, and hard to recognize. I didn't know what was wrong, but I did feel a difference in me. When time did not make the aching for LeeAnne go away, I began to feel bitterness and resentment. It was difficult to recognize because it was not aimed at anything in particular. Each member of my family began to build a wall with very different symptoms showing. They justified their stones, just as I justified mine. Do you imagine the Israelites recognized that their fear and difficulties were separating them from God? Do you think some of our great athletes, movie stars, and leaders have recognized that their obsession with sex, gambling, alcoholism, drugs, or numerous other problems was wall building? Of course not! They saw their lives as basically together, with one small crutch or justifiable need. Unfortunately it is those small stones that build into big walls.

Learn to recognize the symptoms of walling God out. Normal emotions are God-given opportunities for growth, but out of control they become great building blocks. Normal living brings down times, quiet times, discouraging times, and chaotic times to everyone. Yet in all the times of our life, centered on God, the normal ups and downs are balanced by our healthy perspective. When down is where you stay, when your comments are constantly negative, when emotions bring acid into your stomach and bitterness into your heart, you are in trouble. You have become self-centered, not God-centered.

Stones can build from losses, from difficulties, from successes. They can outcrop as biting sarcasm, withdrawal, insecurity, bitterness, rage, depression, or numerous other negative feelings. They can hide under the cloak of superiority or insecurity. If any of the symptoms of spiritual disease are meeting you daily, ask for God's help! Here are some specific signs to watch for:

- One or more out-of-control emotions are a daily part of your life: rage, depression, over-control, worry, fear, bitterness, anxiety, biting sarcasm, rudeness, rancor, irascibility, withdrawal, insecurity.
- Life seems to be a treadmill, a constant catch-up, a get-ahead game.
- You feel all alone, no longer sure that God is real.
- Self-centered attitudes, rather than other-centered attitudes, control your life and focus.
- Life is all serious, with no spontaneous laughter.
- The emotional pain does not stop.
- What other people think is more important than what is right by God's standards.
- Your unhappiness is seen as someone else's fault.

Perhaps you recognize that you are turning inward, building your own wall. You can tear it down simply by saying, "I can't do it alone. Help me!" When you have turned away, finding God again and opening the door of your heart to him will change your life. Through the experience of knowing God, building a wall that separated me from his presence, and then returning to him, I learned a great truth: I can't bear life without God's support; with him I can live with joy, regardless of the holes in my heart. God alive in your spirit is the only answer to deep, abiding joy. Break down your walls, return to God, and live!

Questions

1. What are the symptoms of spiritual disease that indicate you are building a wall to keep God from actively moving in your life?
2. Tell some of the underlying problems that caused people in the Bible stories to begin walling God out.
3. What are some of the unhealthy emotions that warn us we are building walls?
4. Does God *ever* leave us?
5. How do you keep from building walls to lock God out?

Diamonds

◊ *God does not leave us; we wall him out.*

◊ *Age, a history of strong faith, wealth, education—none of these keeps your wall from building if you are self-centered.*

◊ *God, alive in your spirit, is the only answer to deep, abiding joy.*

◊ *Leaving God is usually a subtle and slow process.*

◊ *Wrong actions are a symptom of inner stonewalling.*

◊ *Joy inside is the reason for the happiness outside.*

Life's Flies

THE INSIGNIFICANT
CAN DIM THE POWER
OF THE SIGNIFICANT.

Key to Joy:
Don't be distracted
by the flies of your life.

J spent the evening preparing for an hour-long talk show dealing with the death of a child, in particular, my child. I stayed up most of the night making flip sheets on the topics the show host might cover:

- What was it like to lose a child?
- Was God there?
- What about prayer?
- What happened to our family as we dealt with the death of LeeAnne?
- Were friends helpful or unable to help?
- What would I suggest to others living through a similar experience?

The next morning, the challenge was to resolve all immediate family needs—breakfast, getting the children to school, helping my youngest child settle into a quiet activity—before the ten o'clock program. Radio talk shows are fun, but challenging. This was my first time on radio since the publication of our book *Sunrise Tomorrow*. I needed to be centered, not pulled away by household distractions. An hour can be a lot of time to be ready with instant answers and dialogue via phone. The interview was aired live, so there would be no time for revisions or changing a comment. Pauses in radio interviews are pregnant. People listening anticipate answers; seconds stretch.

Shutting all doors leading to a guest bedroom, I sat down on the floor beside the phone, propping myself up against the bed. I spread the fact sheets around me with only ten minutes until airtime. Ten minutes to quiet my spirit. Radio programs are best when guests sound comfortable and at ease, like a talk between friends on the front porch. As I bowed to ask God's insights and calming influence, a fly flew by. The fly was oblivious to me. He was busy humming, bumping into mirrors, then attacking the windows, back and forth like a kamikaze pilot. I tried to ignore it. I tried to pray through its diving assaults, but when it landed in my hair, the quiet was gone.

I became centered, not on the interview but on killing the fly. With shoe in hand, I leapt over the bed, hit the mirrors, and ran at the walls with no success at doing anything more than irritating the fly. I knew I could not listen to that fly for an hour as I talked. Because of its dodging skills, the fly was winning. I needed a new maneuver, a change of direction. Murder had been unsuccessful. What about simply letting the fly out of the room? The fly was happy with the solution and left willingly, leaving me exactly one minute to pull myself together before the phone rang.

Flies in life are everywhere. Staying centered on God's purposes for our lives is difficult when we are constantly caught by the flies buzzing around us. We are pulled away from the important things in life by thousands of different attackers. Like flies, these nonessential focuses center us

> *Christ's love for us
> is never in question;
> his approval of our actions,
> however, is another issue.*

on the side issues; they create major obstacles; they are, unfortunately, the chief blocks to our developing a deep spiritual relationship with God.

The flies in our lives create these reactions:

- Catch our attention
- Become an irritation
- Shift our focus
- Become a compulsion
- Offer an excuse for failure

Recognizing the Insignificant

Flies don't have to be major life issues such as death, bankruptcy, or divorce. Christ's friend Martha was distracted by flies. Most of us remember sermons on Mary and Martha that said we should strive to be like Mary because she took time to recognize what was important in life.

Martha was too caught up in her own concerns to see the precious gift she had in having Christ in her home. Reading the Scripture I found it interesting that the apostle John said, "Jesus loved Martha and her sister and Lazarus" (John 11:5). I had assumed Christ loved Mary and would love Martha too, if she got her priorities straightened out. I was wrong. Christ's love for Martha was never in question; his approval of her actions, however, was another issue.

What strikes me about the story of Martha and Mary is the simple way a fly can enter your life, even when you are walking with the Lord. The fly craftily captures your attention and leads you from immense happiness to irritation and a self-centered "woe is me" stance. Martha's worthy goal of service to Christ became a problem in her personal relationship with him.

> As Jesus and his disciples were on their way, he came to a village where a woman named Martha opened her home to him. She had a sister called Mary, who sat at the Lord's feet listening to what he said. But Martha was distracted by all the preparations that had to be made. She came to him and asked, "Lord, don't you care that my sister has left me to do all the work by myself? Tell her to help me!"
>
> Luke 10:38–40

Martha was a magnet to people, open, caring, welcoming, and involved in their lives. She welcomed the opportunity to meet Christ's and his disciples' needs in her home with food, rest, and fellowship. But her task became overwhelming as she took her eyes off the reason for her service—fellowship with Christ—and centered on getting the job done. The gift she willingly shared became a fly in her

Our projects should not become more important than our relationships.

life. The problem was not her goodness nor her admirable desire to serve. The problem was that in doing good she had become so sidetracked by the project that she forgot the relationship.

Doing things well is important when you open your home, heart, or talents and assume responsibility for someone or some project. We all want others to think we can handle our jobs well. We need appreciation.

Martha's fly pulled her away from a relationship with Christ to focusing on how to win approval. She became irritable and felt used. Do you find yourself caught like Martha, thrown off your original goal of a deep spiritual walk by the busyness of a project or achievement? Like Martha, you may become caught by insignificant issues that block your accomplishment and center your focus on how much you are giving or doing while others seem to be letting down their end of the bargain.

Like Martha, we all get caught daily by the small, trifling things of life that pull us away from joy and make life seem laborious. Looking at your priorities can help you shift your focus off of the unimportant and move it back to God. Knowing that Christ loved Martha, even when she was blowing it, will encourage you. Christ shared insights into what brings lasting happiness so that we might have abundant life. He does not condemn us for becoming blind to what is important. But he does tell us to open the door and let the flies out of our rooms so that in the quiet we can hear God's voice. Letting the fly out is a key to finding happiness and joy.

We do not want our goal of walking through this life with a joy-filled spirit to be destroyed because our focus is skewed. Our issues can be minor ones that pull us away from centering on the true purpose for life or significant ones that shake us to the core. The size of the pull is irrelevant. Anything that keeps us from centering on life being a gift of God, even in its difficult moments, must be considered a fly.

LeeAnne's death was a major pull in my life. I tried to stay centered on how blessed we had been by her life, how blessed we were to have supportive friends and family, how blessed we were in many other ways, but I hurt so badly. The days grew longer, the nights more filled with aching memories, and my focus centered more and more

---

To not be caught
by the inconsequential,
God demands that we keep our eyes
focused on him.

---

on our loss. I wanted to hang on, dwell in, and surround myself with memories of Lee. Memories were all I had. I would never let them go. Never. If I let them go my little girl would be gone. Fighting with reason, my emotions screamed, *How can you forget? How disloyal for you to even want to move on and leave this part of your life behind!*

LeeAnne was gone physically, but emotionally I clung to her with the tenacity of a child. All my energy was thrust into hanging on to what had been. Death had denied the physical grasp but it could not take away the emotional clutch. We idealized our child, dwelled on the memories, yearned for her, and burdened ourselves with guilt if we allowed the slightest bit of happiness to creep into our corner of depression.

Steps to Positive Focus

1. Stop
2. Think
3. Decide
4. Recenter
5. Move

We had to *stop, think* through our reactions, *decide* to move through our feelings of loss, *recenter* on thanksgiving, and then *move,* one step at a time. It was not easy for us because the tragedy was constantly pulling us down. Yet centering on the right priority was difficult even for Martha, whose problem was simply whether she was carrying too much of the dinner preparation load. Problems come in different intensities, but the choice to quit chasing the fly is always the same, a move to open the door.

Like Martha you and I can be caught by the inconsequential when we become too goal-oriented. Goals in themselves are not wrong. Without goals, apathy and insecurity can warp our lives; yet going off achievement-bound in our own power pulls our eyes away from God, and we deny him the chance to work through us. Mary was praised by Christ, so apparently she was able to balance her goals properly. The balance is tenuous, hard to find, and difficult to keep.

God's guidance is the only way we can balance our commitments, responsibilities, needs, and wants. Faith and flexibility help us adjust and realign our priorities. With the balance that comes from faith, we can keep a sense of joy and expectancy alive in the middle of life's activities. The emotional atmosphere in Martha's home with Christ and his disciples would have been different if Martha had been able to realign her focus from accomplishing her task to enjoying her evening. She reacted to the meal preparation and serving in the same way I reacted to the fly that attacked my hair prior to the radio interview: with irritation. Have you kept your balance? If not, you can shift your focus right now. Chasing flies kills the potential for joy.

Can You Walk on the Water?

The apostle Peter's experience walking to Christ on the water illustrates clearly the power we have while focused on Christ, even in the midst of the storms. Yet, like Peter, the moment we begin to question our power to handle the storm and think about the impossibilities of our efforts, we begin to sink.

> During the fourth watch of the night Jesus went out to them, walking on the lake. . . . "Take courage! It is I. Don't be afraid."
>
> "Lord, if it's you," Peter replied, "tell me to come to you on the water."
>
> "Come," he said.
>
> Then Peter got down out of the boat, walked on the water and came toward Jesus. But when he saw the wind, he was afraid and, beginning to sink, cried out, "Lord, save me!"
>
> Matthew 14:25–30

Keeping your eyes on Christ in the middle of the storm is not easy. You must carefully center your focus and then plot your course for joy, even when you feel the winds and rains buffeting your boat. You must consciously decide to change your course when you see your feet beginning to sink.

After LeeAnne's death, Paul and I knew we needed to pull together because career, home, and family needs combined with loss were a potential threat to our family. Staying close as a family unit would have to be a conscious decision or the problems involved in letting go of someone we loved would split us apart.

To help us stay close, Paul and I chose a hobby, something neither of us had done before so the excitement of discovery was there for both of us. We began to explore the equestrian world with the experienced guidance of breeders and real horse lovers. My love for Paul grew deeper as I watched his enthusiasm and felt his encouragement to come along and be part of this new world with him. We explored mountain trails throughout parks in Tennessee, Virginia, North Carolina, and Kentucky. The beauty and stillness of those trails was broken only by the clomp of our horses' feet. We helped breed the horses, and we watched births. We loaded hay, sheltered the animals from the snow, and watched sunsets as we held out our hands for the horses to eat their grain. Most importantly, we pulled together.

Finding joy as the emotions swell and the goals shift is difficult but not impossible. Our child's death could have been a wedge that divided us as a family, but it didn't! We grew more deeply in love and more committed to family unity than before the crisis. You can let go of the flies in your life that are pulling your life and family apart, too. You can turn around, force yourself away from the flies that have caught your attention, and recenter. You can do as Peter did and reach out for Christ. God may be requiring you to let go of a dream, a relationship, a business, or a goal, but he never requires you to let go of joy.

Questions

1. How can flies mess up our lives?
2. Do problems have to be significant to center our focus on self?
3. What clues will you have that your focus is off balance?
4. What are the five steps to recentering your focus?
5. What creates balance in your life?
6. When we chase the fly or sink in the water, what do we have to do to get help?

Diamonds

◊ *Flies are the insignificant things in our lives that dim the power of the significant.*

◊ *Flexibility is a requirement to walk in faith.*

◊ *God's guidance changes drudgery into joy.*

◊ *God never requires you to let go of joy.*

◊ *The right balance in life comes when God is the focus of our choices.*

◊ *The balance in life is tenuous, hard to find, and difficult to keep as commitments, responsibilities, needs, and wants pull.*

Finding the Why

FINDING YOUR *WHY* IS DEPEN-
DENT ON TRUSTING GOD WITH
YOUR *WHO*.

Key to Joy:
Joy comes when you trust that God
made you who you are for a unique why.

J did not understand some very basic truths about why I am here until I dealt with the entire grief process following LeeAnne's death. Throughout my life, I had been able to hold on in spite of the occasional swirling waters. But after losing Lee, the waves became so high, the waters so turbulent, that I began to drown. Finding that life as I was experiencing it was out of my control, I struggled and fought until finally the depth of emptiness forced me to my knees. I gasped and struggled until, too tired to continue, I cried, "God, help me. Take me where you want me."

Finding your life's purpose, your reason for being, is crucial to happiness. The search for a design, an identity, is perceived by many psychologists as the number-one drive within personality. We want to know there is a reason for life. You and I know that happiness is a fleeting emotion, so unless we understand who we are and trust God with our life direction, we will find ourselves overwhelmed by the bumps and rocks of life. Life will be a desperate search for identity and purpose.

Trusting God is crucial to finding joy because it frees us to see all our life experiences as relevant, shaping us for a unique mission. We recognize growth is transpiring and see that good can flow from every part of our lives, even the failures. We see God growing us. Could it be within God's design for my life that I should have my child for a short seven years? Could it be within his design for you to have been born into a limited, challenged body? Could it be a gift to be raised in an abusive family?

Maybe God's perception of difficulty, challenges, and tragedy is very different from ours. I do know that from the greatest tragedy of my life, the loss of my daughter, has come the greatest blessings of my life. I do know that LeeAnne's life touched and inspired others, because people saw her bubbly radiance and yet knew that she had every reason to be self-centered and whiny with her health difficulties. I do know Dad's laughter and strength throughout his battle with cancer gave tremendous witness to those around him of the choice we have to live with joy, regardless of life's slams. From the very things we consider curses, God can bring great blessings that can help give reason and direction to our lives.

Life Challenges—Opportunities or Curses?

The parable of the talents gives us some basic truths that help us gain insight into the way God views our life challenges. You may find parallels to your own struggle to find your purpose for life.

Again, it will be like a man going on a journey, who called his servants and entrusted his property to them. To one he gave five talents of money, to another two talents, and to another one talent, each according to his ability. . . .

After a long time the master of those servants returned and settled accounts with them. The man who had received the five talents brought the other five. . . .

The man with the two talents also came. "Master," he said, "you entrusted me with two talents; see, I have gained two more. . . . "

Then the man who had received the one talent came. "Master," he said, "I knew that you are a hard man. . . . So I was afraid and went out and hid your talent in the ground. . . . "

His master replied, "You wicked, lazy servant!"

Matthew 25:14–26

From this parable we can infer five basic truths.

1. Everyone has gifts.
2. Each person's responsibility is to use his or her gifts.
3. The master's view of gifts is different from the servant who has not learned to trust him.
4. The difference between the servant who uses his or her gifts and the one who does not is an attitude of trust.
5. The servant who uses his or her gifts will reap a sense of joy and more gifts.

The parable of the talents is a reality-based tale: Life is not fair; some of us have less and bear more than others.

Happiness is a decision to trust that God has a purpose!

Looking at the disparity, you may be thinking, *But Lord, if you had given me more abilities, a better family, a happy marriage . . . I could be happy. Why did you give so much to the oth-*

ers and so little to me? Your soul may be shouting like the man who received only one talent from his master, *My load is too great, my burden too heavy. I have not received a fair share!*

Letting go and trusting God is not easy when the world seems to be falling apart around you. How is it possible to find joy when you have the bad end of the stick? I wanted to know the difficulties I was suffering were for some important reason. Yet no one feels their hardships are important enough to warrant the pain. *Lessons could be learned easier ways,* our emotions argue. Happiness is a decision, in spite of the pain, to trust that God has a purpose!

Use What You Have

Sometimes we find ourselves thinking that the problems in our lives will prevent God from working through us. God is not looking for perfectly together people; he is looking for people who are willing to listen for his voice and use what he has given to them.

The master in the parable of the talents demanded that each servant use what he had been given. The problem with the man who had only one talent was not the gift; the problem was the servant did not know the master. The issue for the master was never one of equality. He made no attempt to equalize his distribution of property. He made no issue

The problem in our life is not the gift; rather, we do not know the Master.

of the dollar return on his property. The amount of the talent, the type of talent, or the return on the talent was not his concern. The issue was more fundamental: trust. The servants who trusted him would reach out to use their gifts. The ones who did not trust would be paralyzed by fear, comparisons, and anger. The master's concern was where his servants put their trust.

The servant with only one talent was focused on himself. Centered on self, the "if only's" become a plague! *If only I had been given more; if only I were more talented; if only I can lie low, my master won't be critical.* The "if only's" began to change to "why me's?" *Why did my master only give me one talent? Why am I expected to carry such a heavy load on such a limited gift? Why should I risk what I have for someone else?* Justification set in. Fear entered. Anger began to play. "Woe is me" began to reign.

Comparing himself to others, the servant felt cheated; he felt that the master had been unjust. Comparisons kept pulling his focus back to self. No one could expect a man given only one talent to be as productive as the others. Simply hanging in there should be enough required of those who were given so little.

Equality is a human idea. You are *not* equal; you are unique, created for a specific purpose, a purpose that only you can fulfill. Comparisons keep us bound and limited. God is never concerned with fairness as judged by a human standard that sees one man with five talents, one with three, and one with one. His eyes see only your using what you have been given, trusting him, so that you can be entrusted with more. He does not look down on you and say, "Poor you. You have so much less than your neighbor. You do not need to worry about using your gifts and enjoying this life. Your reward will be in the afterlife if you simply bear up and suffer in this life." Absolutely not! He cries out, "Use what you have and be happy!" God did not excuse our family from enjoying the rest of our lives after LeeAnne's death. He demanded that we refocus from loss to blessings—how blessed we were to enjoy Lee for almost seven years; how blessed we still are. Our life conditions should not control our choosing joy.

It is important to understand that even if we fail to act with joy under the load of our perceived burden, God continues to love us. God's love is unconditional and is not diminished even if you choose to move away from him. However, because he sees your potential, he wants to free you, to fill you with peace, to cut your chains so that you can be used to share his love. Freed, you radiate happiness; captive to performance, you sow harshness.

Though God's love is unquenchable, regardless of your mistakes, he does hold you accountable, as he did the servants in the parable. The difference between accountability and love can be illustrated by a mother's reaction to her child when he runs into the street. Knowing her child's curiosity, she is not shocked, disappointed, or hurt, but because she loves him, she must hold the child accountable for his actions in order for the child to mature. As the master in the parable held his servants accountable and then meted out rewards, so God holds us accountable for what he has given us.

Our child's death was a time of accountability for us. God undergirded us as we struggled to trust him in our crisis. Choosing to believe there was a purpose for LeeAnne's death was an issue of faith. Emotions demanded we wallow in our grief and cry out, "Why me?" but we fought through them with prayer, the support of friends and family, determination, and trust in God's will.

Joy can take root wherever it is planted. Many times the planting is scary, painful, and dark. LeeAnne's death planted us in the ground. Being in a dark, deep hole is frightening, but with the sunlight's warmth and the gentle washing rains, life begins to flower and bear fruit again. The hardship strengthens and nurtures our faith. Acceptance of God's will for us in all the circumstances of life frees us to bloom where we have been planted.

You May Be Someone's Key to Happiness

You may be the channel of God's love for someone. Love is the key that frees people, not reprimands, not commands, not "you ought to's." We all want to feel understood, or at least accepted if we are not understood. Only after people are loved are they free to change. Had I cried out to LeeAnne when she was a child, wanting to be independent like her friends were, "Lee, you've just got to handle this," she would have yelled back, "Why? No one else has this problem!" Because we cried with her, because we told her we thought she was courageous, because we supported her, she became free to change her attitude, even though she couldn't change her life situation.

I understand tough love. Our responsibility was to help a diabetic two-year-old become an independent, cheerful little child who could feel her life was a treasure, not a handicap. Love demands caring that will help the person stand. There are times to tell someone, "Get up. You must move on!" But you can only say that if you have earned the right, through the love you have shared and wrapped the person in as she was struggling to understand her plight.

You will be called on to be the agent of God's freeing love, to wrap love around someone so God can heal the scars and free his or her heart to soar beyond the hurts of the past or present. Loving someone calls for difficult decisions to discern the difference between a love that allows the "woe is me" attitudes to continue and a love that encourages difficult choices that move one from sorrow to inner joy. Love opens the doors to full use of our potential; failure to love leaves scars. Pray you do not pick up a chisel when God is looking for a soft brush to paint the colors of love. Choosing wisely, you may make the difference as to whether someone can turn loose the hurt and begin to see life as a gift.

Finding Your *Why*

Finding an answer to the "Why am I here?" question involves recognizing that every part of your life has purpose, not just specific portions of it. This spiritual insight frees you to appreciate the growing times, the training times, the friendships, the hardships, and the blessings. Joy bubbles from recognizing your life is filled with talents that can change the world. You can be in bondage to the difficulties in your life or you can soar with enthusiasm above your tethered cords. You don't have to find your *why*—you simply have to be responsible for growing where you are.

What keeps you from seeing the gifts of each moment—unhealthy comparisons, a hurtful past, compulsive problems, a bad marriage, rebellious children? The parable of the talents was written for you. God has entrusted you with talents. You must choose—bury your talents, live with fear and anger because your talent is not what you would have chosen, wrap yourself in a blanket of insecurity, struggle in your own power, or simply trust. When LeeAnne died, we did not perceive her death as offering us opportunities to touch our world. We were overwhelmed, aghast, and empty. It took time to move away from addicting self-pity. How could we appreciate our situation, move out with trust, and feel inner peace and joy? Our reasoning went something like this: Do you believe in God? Sure. Do you trust God? Sure. Are you filled with peace and joy? Absolutely not! How could we be at peace with such loss? We had to choose to turn loose the comparison of what life could have been and what it was. Psychologists call that the grief process; Christians know it is God's healing process.

The decision to be joy-filled is not dependent on life giving you the five talents or your understanding everything that God puts in your path. It is dependent on your accepting who you are because you know your Master. If you are struggling with the inequities in your life, relax. Determine to be happy where you are. You will be amazed at how your life will change as the blessings unexpectedly flow into your soul. Use who you are—be happy!

Questions

1. Why is it important to accept who you are?
2. What difference does trusting God make in our lives?
3. How can you be a light in someone else's search for purpose?
4. When do difficulties become blessings in our lives?
5. What holds you back from trusting God with your life?
6. What is the difference between searching for a life-purpose and seeing life itself as God's purpose?
7. What was the underlying reason for the unhappiness of the man with one talent in the parable?
8. Name specific ways to love someone who is hurting.

Diamonds

◊ *Trusting God is the key to accepting who we are.*

◊ *From life's challenges can come great blessings.*

◊ *Using who you are brings joy into your life.*

◊ *Love opens the doors for us to use our potential; failure to love leaves scars.*

◊ *Comparisons center focus on self.*

◊ *God's greatest miracles are sometimes blessings in disguise.*

Handcuffed on the Inside

8

YOUR INSIDE FINDS A WAY TO
AFFECT YOUR OUTSIDE.

Key to Joy:
Pulling the dirty splinters from your soul
will keep you from locking out joy.

T he stage resounded with cannon fire, swatting swords, and the thump of Long John Silver's peg leg as the marionettes swaggered and pirouetted to the *Treasure Island* tale. In his imagination, eight-year-old Charles was transported to a time of rugged men, ships on the high sea, adventure, and challenge. From that moment, Charles determined to be a pirate. His world was filled with raids, firing cannons, and treasures. Charles's home echoed with vigorous pirate talk and the howling of Bones, his mongrel dog. He wore an eye patch over one eye, held a carefully carved stick-sword, and tied a cut-off broom handle to his leg. With each stride his leg resounded with a loud thump, thump, until the broom handle did what mutilated, thumped, mistreated broom handles have a right to do. It broke, sending a large splinter into Charles's tender skin.

Little boys might cry and run home for help, but not pirates. When the splinter refused to budge, Charles simply pushed it deeper into the skin: Out of sight, out of mind. Charles learned the hard way that ignoring a problem does not make it go away. The buried splinter began

---

If you don't feel an underlying sense of joy permeating your spirit, then you probably have splinters.

---

to fester and within days the courageous pirate was only a little boy with tetanus poisoning. Like Charles, if we fail to care for the splinters that come through our life experiences, they will cause poison that festers and destroys. Splinters that are allowed to fester cause toxic emotions and faulty reasoning that handcuff us on the inside and lock our joy.

Balancing Emotions and Reason

To stay in control of your life, you must recognize the need for a healthy balance between reason and emotion, and then keep the splinters from poisoning it. Healthy reason balances emotion's pulls with logic's quiet strength. Unhealthy reason is rigid, lifeless, compulsive, and controlling. Healthy emotion brings laughter, tears, sunshine, enthusiasm, sadness, and a richness to the texture of our lives. Unhealthy emotions can trap us in emotional pain.

Why would you allow either reason or emotions to drive your decisions if you understand the many problems that imbalance causes? Easy, the double d's, difficulty and desire, team up. Difficulty intensifies and strengthens the emotions' power over reason. Desire pleads, and reason that is not centered in God sees nothing wrong in allowing emotions to take over the playground of the mind. Appeasing the demands of your emotions brings immediate gratification, but if reason and God's principles have been left out, you have created a splinter that is going to infect your system.

Pulling the splinters out is crucial. To pull the wedge out means you must face that it is there. You must see yourself realistically. How do you know you have splinters? If you don't feel an underlying sense of joy permeating your spirit, or if the dampness in your heart is spreading criticism and anger in your world, then you probably have splinters. The theological term for pulling out the splinters is repentance. The elements are simple to state but incredibly hard to employ. First you must face the truth as you seek the root of your actions; then, you must dislodge the splinters.

Understanding three principles about reason and emotions will make it easier for you to temper their relationship.

1. Balance must exist between emotion and reason before they can work together to bring happiness.
2. Emotion and reason must be based on God's principles to bring happiness.
3. A healthy partnership between emotion and reason is a conscious choice.

I thought the choice to live with joy was impossible when LeeAnne died. Death seemed easier than facing the grief emotions. But I knew, deep down, because God's voice was whispering, that if I ever wanted the pain to go away I would have to confront and care for it. I did what

I had to do to survive, and then one step at a time, I began to live again inside.

Easy? Restoring the balance of emotion and reason during that painful time was the hardest thing I have ever done. You may be saying, "But you had other reasons to

---

All emotions are God-given and godlike.

---

live—your husband and your other children—I have none." You are wrong. We all have life, the most precious gift of all, and it can be blessed, wonderful, sunshine-filled, and brimming with laughter. But you have to choose that attitude. If you want joy in your life, you will have to work hard to restore the crucial balance between emotion and reason. Look at the problem:

- Reason is farsighted; emotions are nearsighted.
- Reason can delay satisfaction if it is best for the long term; emotions want instant gratification.
- Reason works by your choice; emotions are spontaneous.
- Reason is difficult to employ; emotions are easy to follow.
- Reason is strong only when joined by your will; emotions are strong on their own.

It is easy to see why a healthy balance is so difficult to achieve.

All healthy emotions can become unhealthy if they remove God-centered reason from the balance. Emotion that outweighs reason creates havoc. A healthy emotion turned unhealthy can become a drive. For example, think about the emotion *happy* out of control. When it becomes a drive, it says, *If you are not happy, your life is worthless.* This creates the treadmill of *happy* commands, *Do whatever is necessary to be happy!* Reason begins to take second place to the drive. We can play the same healthy vs. unhealthy, toxic game with other emotions.

Emotion	Healthy	Unhealthy
Happiness	Springs from joy	Drives need for more and more happiness
Peace	Born from right priorities	Drives need to seek peace in wrong places
Anxiety	Brings awareness and action	Produces pacing and fruitlessness
Sadness	Builds appreciation for good moments	Leads to depression
Anger	Causes positive change	Leaves one raving and powerless
Fear	Opens mind to reality	Leads to paralyzing inactivity

Perhaps you are fighting emotions that have grown into unhealthy, festering splinters. You may have forgotten the source of the anger, frustration, resentment, or depression. But whatever caused the splinter, it is blocking your laughter and locking you into patterns that destroy joy. Ask God's help. Take responsibility for your attitudes. Make sure emotions bow to reason. Hold yourself accountable.

Let go of the pride and pull the splinters. Reclaim the good gift that God meant emotions to be.

Emotions—God's Good Gift

All emotions are normal, natural, and good because they are God-given and godlike. The truth that your emotions are designed by God and are like his own emotions is worthy of your intense study. This understanding can free you from unnecessary guilt when you experience normal emotions. It can free you to love our God who longs for us, hurts when we fail, and wants us to be happy! He is the Alpha and the Omega and yet the Scriptures say he experiences emotions, just as we do. God grows angry, sad, impatient, jealous. He rages, hurts, longs for relationships. (I thought about God's longing as I was longing for my little girl.) He evaluates his actions and changes his original decisions. (Think about the flood, Sodom and Gomorrah, Nineveh.) He feels joy and forgives. Something must be good about *all* of my emotions if our perfect God experiences them too.

For blessings to actualize, trusting God is mandatory, even when he seems quiet.

God expresses many emotions in Scripture. On your own, study the Bible, writing down in a notebook the emotions God experiences as he deals with man. Go deeper. Great lessons are to be learned through scriptural study. Knowing that God has emotions makes him more reachable and encourages us to adore and love him as we build a relationship with him. The emotions you have are not wrong; the wrong comes when you do not overcome emotion's pull to self-focus. God experiences the emotions of anger, hurt, rage, love, longing, and so on, but he is able to forgive and let go, so that he does not bind his Spirit in guilt and seething anger. He is free to feel joy and radiate a love of life. If we see how God lets go, we will learn to become free also.

For now, look at these few selected Scriptures. What emotion is God showing in each? How can he embody some of these emotions and still be God? What does this say to you about your emotions?

- *Grief:* "'The LORD was grieved that he had made man on the earth, and his heart was filled with pain" (Gen. 6:6).
- *Sorrow and regret:* "The LORD smelled the pleasing aroma and said in his heart: 'Never again will I curse the ground because of man, even though every inclination of his heart is evil from childhood. And never again will I destroy all living creatures, as I have done'" (Gen. 8:21).
- *Balances work and rest:* "By the seventh day God had finished the work he had been doing; so on the seventh day he rested from all his work" (Gen. 2:2).
- *Enjoys accomplishment:* "God saw all that he had made, and it was very good" (Gen. 1:31).
- *Anger:* "Then the LORD's anger burned against Moses . . . " (Exod. 4:14).
- *Desires praise:* "But I have raised you up for this very purpose . . . that my name might be proclaimed in all the earth" (Exod. 9:16).
- *Longs:* "I long to redeem them, but they speak lies against me" (Hosea 7:13).
- *Expresses pleasure in others:* "You are my Son, whom I love; with you I am well pleased" (Mark 1:11).

- *Faithful:* "Your love, O LORD, reaches to the heavens, your faithfulness to the skies" (Ps. 36:5).
- *Forgives:* "For I will forgive their wickedness and will remember their sins no more" (Jer. 31:34).
- *Yearns:* "'My heart yearns for him; I have great compassion for him,' declares the LORD" (Jer. 31:20).
- *Expresses sadness:* "Jesus wept" (John 11:35).
- *Overwhelmed by emotions:* "Then he said to them, 'My soul is overwhelmed with sorrow to the point of death . . .'" (Matt. 26:38).
- *Feels alone:* "About the ninth hour Jesus cried out in a loud voice, 'Eloi, Eloi, lama sabachthani?'—which means, 'My God, my God, why have you forsaken me?'" (Matt. 27:46).

Reason—Steadiness for Painful Emotions

Sometimes we question our faith when we find ourselves surrounded by painful emotions. Even as we watched LeeAnne's life ebb away, we knew that God was in control. Faith is a walk based on knowledge that God guides, cares, and has our ultimate good in his design; it is not based purely on feelings. There is no reason to doubt your faith when emotions spiral if you recognize the emotions as normal with great potential for blessing. Yet trusting can be difficult as the pain throbs and emotion asks reason, *Why believe? Where is God anyway?* For blessings to actualize, trusting God is mandatory, even when he seems quiet.

We do not stay on an even keel through life's ups and downs. Emotions ebb and flow; they travel on waves, peaking, crashing, flattening, and then building again for the same agitating actions. Unexpected hurts hurl you back into the swelling stream of emotions over and over. Understanding the fluid nature of emotions makes the fluctuations and repetitions less threatening. The hit-and-run nature of emotions allows coping skills to regroup and the mind to momentarily escape the intensity. Reason keeps nudging and working with emotion, quietly and behind the scenes, *if* you listen. It helps to understand five key emotions that vie for control when difficulties come our way. Expect them. Then you can work through their pulls.

Loneliness

As painful emotions assault, you may feel that no one else in the world has ever had the same problem. A sense of isolation fills your soul. "I can't" takes control. You feel as if you can't do anything. Why? Because isolating emotions make you feel naked and vulnerable. By working through the emotion that cries out, *I'm all alone; I'm different; no one knows how I am feeling,* you grow the healthy realization that you are God's child. You can do anything with God's help because you are never all alone!

Confusion

Intense emotions make you feel confused and crazy. You don't feel normal—and for awhile, you aren't. You can't think; vocabulary is jumbled; memory is defunct; sleep is gone; the mind is detached. Emotions swing from intense pain to numbness. Confusion rains tears. Yet feeling crazy *is* a blessing. It keeps the full thrust of the intense emotions at bay, allowing them to come in small doses.

Anguish

Emotional pain is real. Pain hurts. When LeeAnne died it felt like a knife was tearing out my insides. Sometimes the emotions didn't rip, they swelled, until my body was bursting. My soul filled until a low wail erupted. Torment, affliction, agony, suffering, misery, distress, heartache, sorrow, woe—no word seems adequate. Emotional pain can drive hunger, disrupt sleep, dull the mind, cause illness, or erupt in a thousand ways. However, as you release the emotions and work through their sticky webs, you find that empathy has been birthed. You would not have chosen the route to understanding, but it can bless your life by allowing you to minister to others.

Guilt

Guilt comes packaged with intense emotions. The more intense the emotions, the more encompassing the guilt. If you hold on to guilt, it cripples your spirit, negatively affecting all your responses. Guilt has the greatest potential for blessing if it is used as a tool for growth.

Yearning

Yearning is the most difficult emotion to overcome. Who could be normal after surviving whatever it is that you're yearning for—a lost love, a bungled opportunity, financial devastation, the death of a loved one, divorce, children who have strayed? To give up yearning means you must take responsibility for your own happiness again. You can't blame something outside yourself for your misery. How blessed life becomes when you recognize it is God that fulfills your need.

Guilt and yearning work in partnership—both wrap, cocoon, and encapsulate. When toxic, they offer an excuse for failure; they want pity; they require giving up. They cry out, *Stop trying. Be sad forever!* Together, guilt and yearning demand that you either resign or take control, allowing nothing to affect you so devastatingly again. Both resignation and overcontrol kill joy as they negatively affect you, your family, and your friendships.

Under God's guidance the potentially toxic emotions of guilt and yearning can become two of your most valuable tools for growth and joy. Throughout most of life we focus on how we have been wronged by others, but when guilt and yearning come, the focus centers on self: "What could I have done differently?" Insights can couple with forgiveness, turning the guilt and yearning into a blessing that teaches appreciation for each moment and each relationship of life.

I had to quit yearning for LeeAnne in order to remember the times we had together and the fun memories. As long as I was centered on my loss, yearnings caused my soul to cry out, *Don't stop hurting! Happiness will mean you have forgotten your little girl!* To stop hurting made me feel guilty. Happiness came when I focused on the blessings LeeAnne brought into our lives while she was with us. Focused on thanksgiving, I can remember LeeAnne. So many special times now can refill my thoughts, such as the afternoon LeeAnne held the dance recital at bay until I arrived from picking up our son Paul at the high school. "You can't start until my mom gets here," LeeAnne pleaded. So Sheila Cox, the dance instructor at Bolding School of Dance, delayed the recital until we arrived. How sad it would be to have to bury those special memories!

The Challenge of Control

Learning to control painful emotions that destroy joy is not easy. I have the utmost respect for my father, who taught us how control allows you to handle life with joy and face death with dignity. We watched his determination to rebuild and heard him whistle as he struggled to build stamina: a few steps, a few feet, slowly around the block, and finally, several miles a day.

How he inspired, even in his weakness. Was it easy? Heavens no! There is nothing easy about forcing yourself to live, in spite of emotion's demand to quit. Dad chose to live happy in spite of his circumstances, within his circumstances, and above the pull of his circumstances.

Dad deserved our pity, but he wanted none of it. He knew what you and I should know: Pity never brings joy, only excuses and failure. Happiness and the desire for pity never occupy the same soul. Pity digs a pit to bury happiness. Pity tells us to continually grieve for what we have lost, to focus on the injustice and unfairness. But the truth is, until we control our grieving for what is no more, we will not be free to remember the blessings of the treasure

*If you reach out to him,
God will guide you to joy.*

we held. Dad did not center on what he had lost—his health. Certainly, he was sad about it, but he chose to focus instead on his gratitude for the great health he had enjoyed at other times in his life. He was thankful for the days that he had been given, even pain-filled days.

"Give thanks in all circumstances" (1 Thess. 5:18) is a biblical injunction that requires great faith. It is also a key to our psychological makeup that prevents simmering emotions and bitterness. Emotions are born neutral, but as we have seen, they can grow healthy or unhealthy depending on where you choose to focus. It does no good for me to think my path is harder than yours, my loss greater. The same situations will exist whether you are happy inside or unhappy. Give yourself the gift of joy. Don't let your problems, busy schedule, hectic life, commitments, or failures pull you down. No one can *make* you happy or unhappy; that choice belongs to you. If you reach out to him, God will guide you to joy.

Allowing God to guide will create balance. We have seen that balance is a key to joy. Too much or too little emotion, too much or too little reason can handcuff your joy and keep you captive to the woes of life. The teeter-totter is in tenuous balance as our spirit wages war with our humanity. You must choose to maintain balance.

No one finds happiness by chance. Abraham Lincoln summed it up when he said, "People are about as happy as they make up their minds to be." You hold the controls. Understand the pull of the emotions, accept God's principles as the basis for reason, and then move, a step at a time, to free yourself.

Questions

1. What is the difference between our natural response to emotions and the response we make with God's guidance?
2. How do emotions become toxic? How do emotions become blessings? Give examples.
3. What is a splinter? How do you pull splinters from your heart? How have splinters affected your life?
4. What is the key to knowing you have splinters?
5. Explain how emotions are both God-given and god-like.
6. Compare reason to emotion.
7. What does it mean when we say, "I *have* emotions, but I *am not* my emotions?"
8. How do the double d's, desire and difficulty, affect our emotions and reason?
9. How does guilt and yearning's partnership become a toxic agent or a blessing?

Diamonds

◊ *Yearning offers an excuse for failure, demands guilt, wants pity, and requires giving up.*

◊ *Emotions are born neutral, but they can grow either healthy or unhealthy.*

◊ *People are as happy as they make up their minds to be.*

◊ *Ways to escape dealing with emotions seek you; you must seek healthy coping techniques.*

◊ *Failure to assume responsibility for your splinters causes emotions to grow ugly.*

◊ *Emotion or reason that is out of balance can handcuff you.*

◊ *Pity and joy never occupy the same soul.*

◊ *Reason that is not centered in God sees nothing wrong in bowing to feelings.*

◊ *The battleground upon which normal emotions change to toxic emotions is the mind.*

◊ *Joy demands understanding, accepting, and moving.*

When You Can't Pray Anymore

9

WHEN THE PIECES DON'T FIT,
GOD MAKES THE DIFFERENCE.

Key to Joy:
Happiness is not the absence of problems; rather, it is trusting in the midst of problems.

*M*y husband, Paul, and I were in Bergen, Norway, when the tall ships, racing between different ports in Europe, arrived in this renowned fishing village on the North Sea. Strolling around the docks, we beheld the great windjammers, magnificent reminders of a past full of romance and robust adventure. Passing the Russian windjammer *Norensky*, we were drawn by the crowds around a photographic display in the city's visitor center. Bergen had sponsored a photo contest that obviously had captured the imagination of the passersby. Each entry depicted the theme "Peace."

The third-place winner was a picture of a typical Norwegian church, with huge forest pines in the background and a carved wooden fence, all blanketed by a newly fallen snow. The moonlight was glistening on the snow, lending an air of quiet. Stillness, unbroken silence, solitude, and contentment emanated from the scene. No question, peace was depicted in the photograph.

The second-place winner was another scene of tranquillity. A bubbling brook slowly meandered through a lush forest with one leaf frolicking in the current. You could sense the damp moistness of the woods, the moss on the rocks, the absence of noise, the sparkling light, and the play of shadows on the water. The photograph pulled you to quiet times, to moments of well-being, to a place with no hustle and bustle, to a life without time constraints, to joy-filled freedom from responsibilities and commitments. Watching the crowd, you could feel their response to the second-place winner: right on target.

The photograph that won first place was a scene of a rushing waterfall, a powerful careening river that fell violently to the tumultuous waters below. On a limb protruding from the edge of the waterfall was a small bird in its nest. The bird was sleeping with its wing covering its head. Peace in the midst of turbulence.

Peace on the Inside

Peace is more than outward circumstances; peace comes from the inside out. Inside peace grows from a security that emanates from trusting the limb that holds your nest in the middle of life's waterfalls. Peace when life is raging is indisputable peace.

When one is confronted with problems, the decision to live in peace, as opposed to worry and frustration, is a conscious one that requires courage and faith. Dad and LeeAnne had to choose to trust that all of life has a purpose—the good times, the quiet times, the difficult times, and the turbulent times. They had to choose to rest in the nest, out on a limb, with the spray and roar of the waterfall constantly reminding them that fear was nearby if they wanted to give in to it. The good news is that once the decision had been made to rest in the security of the nest, they were no longer captive to the dangers and demands of the

*Peace is more than outward
circumstances;
peace comes from the inside out.*

swirling, turbulent waters. The peace abiding within their spirits freed them to rest on the limb.

The choice to trust frees you from bondage. The choice allowed LeeAnne and Dad to *have* a disease, but not be identified *by* the disease. Dad had cancer; he was not cancer. LeeAnne had diabetes; she was not diabetes. Taking the reins allows your spirit to soar with joy, even with the problem. If the disease, problem, sour relationship, or sin takes the reins, you feel like a helpless victim of circumstances. The powerlessness of your situation exists in your mind, not in reality. You may die from cancer, but it can never steal your inside peace, unless you allow it to.

I can hear you now screaming "BUT!!!" "But if you only knew what I have to live with!" "But if you only knew how shortchanged I have been by God!" "But if you only knew what I endured as a child!" "But who could be happy with all this trash I bear?" The Israelites screamed "but" loud and long. In the desert the Israelites protested "No way! I'm not going a step further." How did Moses hang on as leader when complaints, grumbles, rebellion, disgruntled participation, and questioning of his every action dogged his footsteps? He knew who was in charge.

Who's in Charge?

Uncertainty was the crux of the Israelites' problem in the desert. Without knowing who was in charge or what the social structure would be, without rules or guidelines, how could anyone feel they had a handle on life? Talk about trusting God is one thing; trusting is quite another, especially when the torrents of the waterfall rage below. The Israelites were left without any of the normal things that give us a sense of security—home, neighborhood, career, routines—so fears, worries, anxieties, grumbling, and complaining were a natural outgrowth. Life in the desert meant they had to trust God's leadership completely. Letting go and trusting God, who is up there, somewhere, can be very frightening, but if we take the risk, God's inner guidance produces a quiet spirit. When we are filled with God's Spirit, peace reigns, even in the midst of the world's woes.

Who you choose to be in authority will determine whether your life will be peace-filled or turbulent. If you choose to follow your human nature, you will give in to what you feel. Giving in to your desires may feel good and provide instant gratification, but it is only temporary happiness. Following your spiritual nature often counters wants and desires, but it is the only way to lasting happiness.

How do you make sure your spiritual nature stays in charge? Get quiet! Being quiet is *listening* for God's insights before you start off to *do* anything. Listening may lead you to continue with purposeful, directed activity, or it may lead you to leave your safe harbor to go into the uncharted waters. Quiet is a spiritual quality that produces an inner peace that cannot be shaken in any outside circumstances. God's Word says, "In quietness and trust is your strength" (Isa. 30:15). To get quiet does not mean you don't do anything because you are afraid of doing the wrong thing. To get quiet means you *act*, trusting God to help you find purpose and direction.

We all know how hard choosing to be quiet in the midst of challenges can be. The quiet attitude requires that we:

- Choose Christ as the authority of our lives.
- Accept ourselves as worthy children of God, with purpose and design.
- Recognize God-given emotions so that we do not allow them to control us, overwhelm us, or frighten us.
- Choose to focus on thanksgiving.
- Wait on the Lord for insights and instructions within our spirit.

Singing the Right Song on the Right Side of the Water

In Exodus 15, Moses and the Israelites sang a song to the Lord. They praised and exalted him, thanking him for opening the Red Sea and hurling Pharaoh's horses and riders into it. They were ecstatic and in awe of his majestic power and wonders. The problem was that the Israelites sang the *right* song but it was on the *wrong* side of the waters. They had a trust crisis.

God needed to remind the Israelites of his power, his hand on their lives, his love, and his ability to lead them to freedom. The Israelites had seen his miracles of plagues and torment that had impelled Pharaoh to release them from slavery. Yet believing he was leading them and acting on that belief were two different matters. When the reality of the Red Sea stood between them and freedom, with Pharaoh's armies chasing them down, they cried out to Moses.

> As Pharaoh approached, the Israelites looked up, and there were the Egyptians, marching after them. They were terrified and cried out to the LORD. They said to Moses, "Was it because there were no graves in Egypt that you brought us to the desert to die? What have you done to us by bringing us out of Egypt? Didn't we say to you in Egypt, 'Leave us alone; let us serve the Egyptians'? It would have been better for us to serve the Egyptians than to die in the desert!"
>
> Exodus 14:10–12

God parts the Red Sea; the Israelites safely cross; he closes it on the Egyptians. Miraculously saved, they sing in praise. Too often we do the same thing. When problems come on us, we moan, wail, and cry out for help, trembling and fearful. We wait to praise God—even though we know of his help in the past—until our problem is resolved. We unnecessarily bear the mantle of anguish. Singing the right song on the right side of the water frees us to experience joy even *before* everything is smooth and easy. We are human but, thanks be to God, we are also filled with his Spirit, which gives us the power to sing and to rest in all the challenges of life.

This, Too, Will Pass

When we are hurting, when it seems too hard to pray, we can all be encouraged by knowing that this, too, will pass. Because we know that Christ is the limb that holds us in the storm, we need to add one more phrase to this truth: This, too, will pass because we are trusting the Master.

The Israelites wandered in the desert for forty years. They prayed fervently to be led to the Promised Land, but their prayers seemed to fly away with the desert sands. Discouraged, they sought a scapegoat as they railed against Moses.

> The whole Israelite community set out from the Desert of Sin, traveling from place to place as the LORD commanded. They camped at Rephidim, but there was no water for the people to drink. So they quarreled with Moses and said, "Give us water to drink."
>
> Moses replied, "Why do you quarrel with me? Why do you put the LORD to the test?"
>
> But the people were thirsty for water there, and they grumbled against Moses. They said, "Why did you bring us up out of Egypt to make us and our children and live-stock die of thirst?"

Then Moses cried out to the LORD, "What am I to do with these people? They are almost ready to stone me."

The LORD answered Moses, "Walk on ahead of the people. Take with you some of the elders of Israel and take in your hand the staff with which you struck the Nile, and go. I will stand there before you by the rock at Horeb. Strike the rock, and water will come out of it for the people to drink."

Exodus 17:1–6

Does God ask us to do the impossible? Of course! Would we ever call on him if we were self-sufficient? God waited until Moses and the entire nation recognized the enormity of their water problem; he watched patiently as Moses exhausted all his resources searching for a solution. Then when Moses cried out, "I can't do this without you," God directed him to do the ridiculous—hit a rock with a staff. Only desperation would have given Moses the courage to do such a thing in front of everyone. How interesting that Moses held the solution to the problem in his hand; yet until he was at his wit's end and sought God's help, he did not recognize it. God was growing up a community of faith. The Israelites needed a generation to grow into an independent nation capable of fighting for its lands, supporting its cities, and trusting in its Lord. The Israelites wanted easy, quick answers, but they grew stronger as they awaited God's timing.

When prayer seems to be rejected and there are no quick answers, we may question our understanding of God and grumble as the Israelites did. We must learn to accept that every situation is within God's design. A proper understanding of prayer can help us do that.

Prayer has three elements: faith, petition, and God's will. Overemphasis on the first two elements, faith and petition, creates misunderstanding. We ignore the third element of prayer: God's will. If the prayer succeeds, we credit the miracle to faith and God's answering our petition. If it

Doing it right is not the only way we learn to trust.

fails, we question whether there was enough sincerity or wonder if we sinned. We forget to consider that God's plan may be different from our petition.

Christ was in perfect communion with God when he prayed that his life be extended. His emotional plea was replete with such urgency and physical exhaustion that the sweat from his brow was like drops of blood. In spite of his agony, he was able to pray, "Yet not as I will, but as you will" (Matt. 26:39). He embodied the three elements of prayer perfectly: faith, earnest petition, and God's will. God's will is the critical factor, because he alone knows the total design of life. As we pray, trusting God's will and keeping our eyes focused on him, our faith grows and our spirit fills with joy to carry us through the difficult times.

Facing Our Red Seas

The moment I learned my two-year-old child was diabetic, I felt like I was standing at a Red Sea. Where was God? LeeAnne had been sick for a couple of weeks. "Just a lingering flu," the physicians surmised. I suspected it was more than that, for every day she grew more lethargic and clingy. Listening to my cries that something was wrong, my physician-husband Paul brought home a testing kit to check LeeAnne's blood sugar level.

God was taking care of us! Had we put LeeAnne to bed that night with her blood sugar level so elevated, she would have been comatose when we tried to awaken her the next morning. We recognized that fact and were grateful, but we were also tremendously alarmed—not only for the present medical needs that LeeAnne would face, but for the dire medical prognosis that hung over her future. Did we simply trust and feel at peace within our hearts? No. We anguished over the loss of her health. We grieved.

The knowledge that our ability to trust grows as we walk through life should encourage you in your Christian journey. The Israelites' years in the wilderness taught them to submit to God's authority. Over and over they failed to trust, but through those very failures, God taught them new lessons in obedience that continued the growth of their faith. Doing it right is not the only way we learn to trust. Quite often our greatest faith-building lessons come when we fail royally, reevaluate, pick up our bruised hearts, and recommit to a deeper walk. Faith grows, staggers, questions, even doubts, but God is always there to welcome us back and encourage us to keep on. Adversity and failure can be powerful lessons in growing trust.

When the waterfalls are roaring, when we face our Red Sea, when we are too discouraged to pray anymore, we must start singing our song, look upward, and rest like the bird, sleeping in our nest with an arm covering our head, because we know the limb is secure.

Questions

1. Have you encountered times when you could not pray? What blocked your prayers?
2. What are the requirements of a quiet spirit?
3. Why was the song of the Israelites a right song sung on the wrong side of the river? Where do you usually sing your song?
4. Is your ability to trust God in all the situations of your life growing? Explain.
5. Illustrate the growing faith walk of a Bible personality. When did the greatest lessons in faith occur—

during the hard times, the easy times, the successes, the failures?

Diamonds

◊ *The source of authority in your life determines your peace and joy.*

◊ *Prayer stops flowing when we stop trusting and rely on our own strength to control life.*

◊ *Failure can be a step in growing faith.*

◊ *God's working within our spirit births a quiet, positive direction and peace inside our hearts.*

◊ *Happiness is not the absence of problems; rather, it is trusting in the midst of problems.*

◊ *The joy choice is the choice to be happy, regard less of circumstances.*

10

Forgiving versus Forgetting

FORGIVENESS IS THE WELL-SPRING OF JOY.

Key to Joy:
Forgive, so it is unnecessary
to forget.

A grandmother in Galax, Virginia, stood in the question-and-answer portion of a seminar we were concluding on death and dying. "Could you help me? I know I must forgive the young man who ran over my three-year-old grandson when he went out to help his granddaddy get the mail from our mailbox. The teenager was busy waving to his friends and didn't even feel his car swerving off the road until it was too late. I know he did not mean to kill Chris, and I think I could forgive him, but he has never apologized, never said anything at all to me. His ducking makes me angry. He owes us at least an apology." She's right. The young man owed the family of the child he killed an apology.

Yet the grandmother was wrong to believe the apology would help her forgive. Forgiveness is unconditional; if a condition must be met, the act changes from *forgiveness* to *forgetfulness*. A precondition never births forgiveness because it places the burden on someone else. If the other person does not act, we can continue to focus our anger on them. But even if they do act, we find that we are unable to forget what they have done. We hold on to our hurt and anger. Attempting to forget how wronged we feel turns the hurt inward, stuffing the pain behind some closed door within the mind, which will fling open each time the memory is triggered.

Though the grandmother thought she could forgive if the teenager apologized, it wouldn't have worked. If the teenager had apologized, her subconscious would have reasoned, *My requirements are met so now I must forgive, but I can't because the hurt is so great, so I will forget how wronged I feel.* Forgetting doesn't work! The mind never forgets; it is a computer that simply stores memories. Forgetting doesn't bring the hoped-for release from the hurt. Stored hurts simmer and periodically resurface, bringing pain each time.

Forgiveness must come without strings attached. Forgiveness will allow you to remember. Though the pain may still be there, the power of seething anger is not. It has been forgiven. You are left with the learning and growth that have transpired by your working through the hurt. It is your choice whether you will choose to live with simmering anger or with the peace of forgiveness. Stated so simply, you would opt for forgiveness and peace, as would everyone else. The difficulty is that forgiving that brings joy is so much harder than forgetting that creates seething. Unfortunately, the easy way out drops stones into your heart.

Stones in the Heart

A sultan of ancient Persia was obsessed with finding the perfect wife. He would give each new bride one thousand nights in which to prove her worthiness. If she failed, he would behead her (Persia's equivalent of a quickie divorce) and begin again. A beautiful and charming young woman was chosen to be the next bride to follow in the line of the king's unsuccessful attempts to find perfection. Reassuring her courtesan father, she shared with him her plan to survive the one thousand nights by spinning stories. Sure enough, each night as she lay in bed she captured the sultan's imagination by the insights woven through her skillful storytelling. She survived the one thousand nights as her husband, the sultan, eagerly awaited each night's new tale. The stories she told were captured for generations to come in *One Thousand and One Nights*.

One of her tales was about a respected businessman in the Persian community who married a beautiful young woman. His first love was his business and he rarely took time to acknowledge that his wife was important to him. In her loneliness, the woman was swayed by the wiles of a young Persian nobleman who was captivated by her beauty and gentility. He pursued and won her neglected love. The husband found his wife in bed with her lover and with great restraint, he resisted killing either the nobleman or his wife.

The community praised the businessman for his caring and forgiving spirit, and everywhere he heard, "What a strong man Omar is to have forgiven his wife when he had every right to have her stoned." With each comment he remembered his wife's indiscretion and disloyalty, and a pebble formed within his heart. Though his wife was never again unfaithful, when Omar looked at her he remembered the affair; when he slept with her he fantasized of his wife with her lover; when she dared to speak her thoughts he reminded her that she was not worthy to speak because of her unfaithfulness. Another pebble formed in his heart with each angry and resentful thought, no matter how kindly expressed. Through the years Omar slowly became hard and cold. It could be seen in his eyes and felt in his attitude. One evening as Omar held his wife, reminding her how much he loved her because he had forgiven her of such a terrible sin, a pebble filled the last remaining space of light in his body and, in her arms, Omar turned to stone.

Omar had expressed words of forgiveness, but he merely stuffed his hurt. Each time someone reminded him of how wonderful he was to have forgiven his wife, he remembered her indiscretion and his anger grew. Each time he held his wife or she failed to meet his standards,

---

God's forgiveness and love free you to forgive and to accept forgiveness from others.

---

he remembered her ill-treatment and the memory added more anger. True forgiveness would have made the indiscretion irrelevant. If someone had reminded him of his wife's cheating, he simply would have regarded it as a time in the past from which he and his wife had grown, an opportunity for him to better understand his wife's needs. He would have been happy that they had weathered the storm together and that their love had grown a deeper commitment. Forgiveness allows growth from the past and prevents stones from forming in the heart.

How Do You Forgive?

The ability to forgive comes from one source: a right alignment with God. Recognizing your need for God's forgiveness and then accepting his love is necessary for healthy self-esteem. If God can forgive you and love you, then you are valuable. God's forgiveness and love free you to forgive and to accept forgiveness from others. Failure to recognize your need for God's forgiveness or to accept his love hardens your spirit. A critical attitude develops that springs against others. Self-focus locks you into attitudes and responses that deepen the hurts and generate a craving for restitution and justice. Negative thoughts snare your mind. A sense of futility and failure, endless fears and insecurities, an unhealthy drive to earn acceptance, and an obsessive need to control nullify happiness.

The story of Joseph is a witness to the joy that forgiveness brings to our lives when bitterness has every right to reign and control. In Genesis we read of Vice-Pharaoh Joseph's testing of his brothers, who did not recognize him to be the brother they had sold into slavery twenty years before. Joseph's servant planted a silver cup in the youngest brother's sack when the twelve brothers were leaving Egypt after purchasing grain for their starving tribe. The brothers pled for Benjamin's release, offering to accept Joseph's punishment in Benjamin's place. Joseph saw their penitent hearts and sent his servants away so he could talk to them in private.

> Then Joseph could no longer control himself before all his attendants, and he cried out, "Have everyone leave my presence!" So there was no one with Joseph when he made himself known to his brothers. And he wept . . . "I am your brother Joseph, the one you sold into Egypt! And now, do not be distressed and do not be angry with yourselves for selling me here, because it was to save lives that God sent me ahead of you."
>
> Genesis 45:1–5

Joseph was able to forgive his brothers because he let go of the chief block to forgiveness—*pride*. He could have justified a grudge: dreams, goals, relationships, his home—all were gone. Yet with God, he managed to refocus and prosper.

He could have simmered and raged at the injustices of his life, blaming his failures on his evil brothers. Joseph chose to dwell instead on God's finding a purpose for him, even in the midst of extreme disappointment and challenges. As he dwelt on God's blessings rather than restitution, God brought joy into his heart. Joy brought an openness and a sense of security that shone in Joseph's life.

Recognizing your need for forgiveness is humbling. *Accepting* it is freeing. *Giving* it cuts the bonds that tie you to injuries, slights, and wrongs. Can you imagine the anger and hurt that Joseph felt when his world was demolished by the rage of his brothers? Yet Joseph grew into a better person after the life-shattering event—a better man, a better friend, and a better leader—because God healed his heart. What about his evil brothers? Joseph recognized that they had grown empathy, sympathy, and caring. Their guilt and remorse had thrown them to their knees where God's forgiving grace had helped them stand again. God's miracle of forgiveness changes you inside out.

Two Lives—One Forgave, One Forgot

Another way to see why forgiveness is crucial to joy is to look at the examples of two lives. Both were tremendously talented, respected individuals, but their reaction to their life difficulties turned one into a victim, the other into a heroine.

Babe Ruth, who won fame as the greatest slugger in baseball history, had been a disregarded, abused child. His parents dumped him at St. Mary's Industrial School in Baltimore with the farewell, "We don't want you, kid. You are too much trouble." He grew up an unloved, unlikable child with one talent that offered him a way out of the ghetto: He could hit a ball. Discovered by the New York Yankees, George Herman Ruth became baseball's heralded hero—

loved, honored, and cherished as the robust, big-hearted, big-sized Babe. The mighty Babe hit 714 regular season home runs in his baseball career, a record for almost forty years until Hank Aaron broke it. A larger-than-life man with a tremendous love for life, the Babe was a national hero for three decades. Yet Babe Ruth could never do enough, be enough, or earn enough to feel good about himself. He sought happiness in wild parties, women, drinking, and gluttony. Adoration, respect, an outstanding career, and wives who tried to love him were not enough to gloss over the unforgiven past. What could have been a storybook success story was a classic epic tragedy caused by unforgiven hurts.

In contrast, Corrie ten Boom chose to forgive those who committed the atrocities in her life, and in doing so, found peace within her circumstances. Her family endured great suffering during World War II because they had sheltered Jewish friends, protecting them from the death squads. Her family was imprisoned at Ravensbruck, one of the most horrid of the concentration camps, where they died and she barely survived. After a clerical error resulted in her release, Corrie ten Boom slowly rebuilt her life in Holland. A renowned speaker, she was invited to speak about God's forgiveness to an audience in defeated Germany.

After her speech was over, a man walked toward her, holding out his hand. She recognized him as one of the most cruel guards at Ravensbruck. In her book *Tramp for the Lord*, she relates the experience.

I was face-to-face with one of my captors and my blood seemed to freeze.

"You mentioned Ravensbruck in your talk," he was saying. "I was a guard there."

"But since that time," he went on, "I have become a Christian. I know that God has forgiven me for the cruel things I did there, but I would like to hear it from your lips as well. Fraulein,"—again the hand came out—"will you forgive me?"

And I stood there—I whose sins had again and again to be forgiven—and could not forgive. Betsie had died in that place—could he erase her slow terrible death simply for the asking?

It could not have been many seconds that he stood there—hand held out—but to me it seemed hours as I wrestled with the most difficult thing I had ever had to do.

For I had to do it—I knew that. The message that God forgives has a prior condition: that we forgive those who have injured us. "If you do not forgive men their trespasses," Jesus says, "neither will your Father in heaven forgive your trespasses. . . ."

"Jesus, help me!" I prayed silently. "I can lift my hand. I can do that much. You supply the feeling."

And so woodenly, mechanically, I thrust my hand into the one stretched out to me. And as I did, an incredible thing took place. The current started in my shoulder, raced down my arm, sprang into our joined hands. And then this healing warmth seemed to flood my whole being, bringing tears to my eyes.

"I forgive you, brother!" I cried. "With all my heart."*

God's grace freed Corrie ten Boom from the agonies locked in her soul because she took the first step to stretch out her hand.

Pride is a major factor that must be overcome in order to forgive. The mind argues, *Why should I forgive? Never! How can I?* You *can* forgive with God's help, and you must forgive, because if you don't you will never be able to release the wrongs. Forgiveness requires a conscious decision. The effort may seem impossible, but if you want to feel joy and freedom within your spirit, you must reach out your hand.

---

* Corrie ten Boom, *Tramp for the Lord* (New York: Fleming H. Revell, 1974), 56–57.

You know the pains you have buried in your heart. Others may see the symptoms, but you alone can find the root and, by the act of forgiveness, destroy the power it has in your life.

Applying the Truths

Do you want to free yourself from the hold of an unforgiving heart? Apply these truths to your actions and they will give you the courage to step toward forgiveness.

You are responsible for you! The most crucial part of healthy emotions is the understanding that the person you are responsible for is you! You are not responsible for the attitudes and responses of other people in your life; you are responsible for *your* attitudes and responses. Quit worrying about someone else. Let go of the expectations you want fulfilled before you are willing to choose happiness. Joy won't spread into your heart until you begin saying, "So be it . . . I am going to be happy regardless. I refuse to hang on, to forget, and stuff my feelings. I will forgive so that I can be free."

No one is grown-up, so be tolerant! You are growing up, but no one is grown-up! Age doesn't make a person grown-up. We spend our lives growing into the kind of people God wants us to be. It is a continuing process that is never finished, for we are always in need of God's guidance and grace. Knowing that no one is grown-up makes forgiving and caring easier.

Accepting and giving forgiveness is a walk in faith. Until you accept that God loves and forgives you, you are unable to forgive yourself and others. The grace to talk to the guard who had a part in destroying Corrie ten Boom's family came *after* she accepted God's forgiveness for the anger and hurts she felt toward those who had so mistreated her. The warmth flowed into Corrie's heart *after* she reached out to shake the guard's hand, not before. Letting go of the anger, pride, and hurts that have festered often comes after the act of forgiving, not before. In accepting and giving forgiveness, we must act in faith that grace and release will come *after* we have forgiven.

Failure is healthy! Success with no failure creates an emotional desert. Drawing closer to God is the goal, not being faultless. Recognizing that God loves us though we are imperfect, we can brush ourselves off and try again . . . and again, and again, as we aim toward perfection in Christ!

Forgiveness requires more than words. Words are meaningless unless they are consistent with life actions. You may say you have forgiven someone, but if you avoid them, grow angry when you are with them, or allow chaos to be part of your relationship, forgiveness is not in your heart. People read forgiveness in attitudes and responses. Through your actions, you can tell others you have accepted God's love and forgiven the hurts of your life.

Hurtful patterns grow from an unforgiving spirit. An unforgiving spirit causes the "Give me! I need! You owe!" demands to power an inside treadmill. Railing, begging, clinging, harboring, criticizing, and pity parties become part of your life pattern. Hurtful patterns build as you live in painful situations. To deal with an unforgiving spirit you must face the truth. Wrong is wrong. Bad actions are bad. Irresponsibility is irresponsibility. You can change if you see that what you are doing is unhealthy, negative, and wrong. You can loosen yourself from the strangling hold of aberrant behavior if you choose to forgive.

Forgiving is a choice. Joy is a choice to process life, in and out. Processing out takes place when we forgive. Joy's choice is simple: harbor or process. Blessings flow when we forgive and deal with life truthfully. Remember:

- We have a choice as to how we will respond to difficulty or blessing.

- We must discern that there are rights and wrongs.
- We must understand wrong choices bring pain, right choices bring blessings.
- We must understand loving others is *in spite of*, not *because of*.
- We can be whole and emotionally healthy.

Perfect homes with perfect love, perfect relationships, perfect health, and wealth exist only in our dreams. As a Christian, though you acknowledge that the past and even present circumstances of life affect you, you affirm that with God's freeing grace, you can choose to forgive and let go of their harmful effect. You can't tiptoe around problems if you want to be free of their control. Blame games may bring restitution but they do not bring peace.

Forgiving takes the punch and power out of the external and allows you to soar in the warmth of God's love. The turning point that allows you to process out the junk that poisons your joy is simply deciding that the negative, hurting, critical spirit within you is no longer acceptable. A bad start, sad years, and hard times are not the end of the world, nor the only option open to you. You can change your life whenever you choose to see it for what it is . . . your life!

You have the key. It is not the forgetting that brings you on the road that leads to joy; it is the forgiving. Forgive yourself. Forgive others. Forgiven, the hard times become growth times. Forgiven, the hard times make the good times more precious. Forgiven, the hard times allow you to feel God's power holding you up. Forgiven, life takes on a special glow from the wellsprings of joy. Forgiven, self-focus transforms into love-focus.

Not many second chances exist in the world today. The pressure is on to be the best and get the most in a dog-eat-dog world. But Jesus offers a second chance—the chance to begin again, to recenter, and move on. If you wonder how God can use you to make a difference in your world, just look at those he has already used and take heart. If his forgiveness can change Joseph and his brothers, he surely can change you and me!

Questions

1. Why is forgiving so hard?
2. How does forgetting, as opposed to forgiving, cause stones to form in the heart?
3. Contrast forgiveness in the life of Corrie ten Boom and Babe Ruth. Are you forgiving or forgetting?
4. What is meant when we say, "Step out in faith"? How did Corrie ten Boom step out in faith when she shook the guard's hand? Describe a time you stepped out in faith.
5. Can you choose your response to the circumstances in your life?
6. What happens when we fail to deal with life truthfully and forgive?
7. When is failing healthy? Share a time you have grown from failure.
8. What understandings free you from an unforgiving spirit?
9. What blessings fill your spirit when you forgive?

Diamonds

◊ *Joy's choice is simple: harbor or process.*
◊ *Forgiving, not forgetting, leads to joy.*
◊ *Forgiveness given with strings attached binds the heart and creates inner desolation.*

◊ *Forgiveness must be given as God gives it—freely.*

◊ *Forgiveness allows growth from the past.*

◊ *Forgiveness flows from right alignment with God.*

◊ *Pride and guilt are the chief roadblocks to forgiveness.*

Discovering the Diamonds

11

A DIAMOND IS A CHUNK OF
COAL THAT BECOMES RADIANT
UNDER PRESSURE.

Key to Joy:
Continuing to grow from difficult times
keeps your eyes filled with wonder and sparkle.

You can find this world to be filled with diamonds, glistening, glimmering, sparkling, no matter how much time you have spent in the muck and mire. All you have to do is start the process, one small step at a time, and let God help you along the way. The starting can be difficult, the process laborious, the thought of wasted time a deep sadness; but the change in your life will kindle life in your spirit.

We do not need to throw away the past—our failures, our hurts from relationships—when we choose to recenter our love and trust in God. Life is not wasted by our mistakes. The past offers us great growth lessons. God uses our trials, pressures, temptations, successes, and relationships, if we let him, to chip away our rough edges and shape us into his diamond. The chipping can be painful, but life with diamond qualities fills our spirit with the ability to shine in the midst of anything life can throw our way.

Nobody grows old by merely living a number of years; people grow old by failing to grow from difficult times. Youth is a temper of the will, a quality of the imagination, a vigor of the emotions, and a freshness that comes from

Love brings trust; trust brings joy.

not being trapped by life's negatives. Years may wrinkle the skin, but to give up enthusiasm is to wrinkle the soul. Whether seventeen or seventy, if there is a love of wonder, an appreciation of each moment, and a childlike excitement for what's next in a person's heart, that person is young. Wonder and love for life grow from letting the good *and* the ugly teach us. The good brings sparkle and enthusiasm; the bad brings an opportunity to grow.

A friend sent me a birthday card: *I see you are still smiling. You must not understand the situation.* I used to look at my father and wonder if, like the card expressed, he really understood life. He never spoke a bad word about anyone. Social position, status, degrees, nothing seemed to ruffle his feathers or threaten his manhood. Was it innocence that seemed to blind his eyes to the worst sides of humankind? I wondered if LeeAnne was too young to know that she was choosing to be so happy. I watched her twirl and laugh, giggle with her freedom and joy, even though she didn't feel well most of the time.

I loved the card, but I *do* understand. My father and LeeAnne both found joy in life because they used God's strength, not because they were naive or had carefree lives. Their spirits soared with enthusiasm because they chose

*Our gift from God is who we are; our
gift to God is what we become.*

to trust that their lives and experiences were not a mistake.
With trust, they felt God's support. From love came trust;
with trust came joy.

This is your life. You can blame your unhappiness and
lack of zip on someone else, on life being unfair, on the
overload, the pressure, or the prejudice. You can justify
your anger because you did not have a good start; your
parents were bums; your looks are disgusting; your health
is a wreck; your friends are all louses; your spouse is a
cheat; your children are troublemakers. You can make any
excuse for your negative attitude, but I will counter, "You
can be happy if you choose!"

Choose to be happy with who you are, where you are,
and what you have. Start right now. The choice to process
life in and out, as opposed to harboring seeds of discon-
tent, will free you. You can do it! The reward will be a life
filled with joy. Imbed the keys of joy into your heart so they
become a part of your automatic actions. When your focus
goes astray, forgive yourself, learn, and begin again.

I took my son Brad for a hamburger yesterday. A
teenager who had cerebral palsy was working there. Brad
had never seen anyone working with a challenged body
before, so I explained the cause and the difficulties involved
in living with the disability. Brad watched and then said,
"Mom, he seems so happy!" What an opportunity to share
insight with Brad that someone had helped this teenager
see his possibilities instead of his impossibilities. I explained
that we all face different trials—the unfortunate, the tragic,
the difficult, and the challenging. But if we choose to focus

on the possibilities, as this young man who was busily and cheerfully working had done, we can rise above the trials and be a joy-filled influence on the world.

Diamonds in the Making

Let's take a quick overview of four very different ways God sculpts diamonds. Using four Bible personalities, we will see how real people with real problems grew and learned to trust as God chiseled them into priceless gems. On your own, you may want to study in greater detail the way they grew to shine in their world. Tell their stories to your children. Make them alive. Help your family understand that God had a plan for Joseph, Paul, Ruth, and Abraham, just as he has for each of you.

> My frame was not hidden from you
>   when I was made in the secret place.
> When I was woven together in the depths of the earth,
>   your eyes saw my unformed body.
> All the days ordained for me
>   were written in your book
>   before one of them came to be.
>
> Psalm 139:15–16

Share with your children the major challenges that led these four heroes of the faith to discover that life *without* God is just life; life *with* God is abundant. Share their struggle to keep centered on God when the storms of life came their way. Emphasize the process of growth through failures and successes, good and bad choices, and a fluctuating walk with God.

Joseph: Great Tragedy

Joseph was born to fulfill a great task for God: the saving of many lives from famine through his insight and leadership. Early in his life, he sought God; but granted a vision of his blessed future, he repelled his brothers with his obnoxious behavior. They determined to kill him, but instead sold him into slavery.

From wealth to slavery was a long slide in human terms, an epic tragedy for a seventeen-year-old. Through Joseph's battle with loss, hurts, and anger, God began to chisel away rough edges, and Joseph's brilliance began to shine. He chose to believe that God could use the evil of his brothers' deception to bring good within his life. He kept his heart centered on God's love and laws as he let go of rejection and loss.

Joseph knew that God's will is the critical thread of life. Because God cares, we simply must trust and allow him to use us. Trusting like Joseph, we are freed to soar with joy, even within the prisons of life.

Joseph's gift of discernment was the vehicle that brought him out of prison and into the royal courts to interpret the puzzling dreams of Pharaoh. Recognizing the dream to be a vision of a coming famine, Joseph proposed a plan that would make Egypt the grain market for the Eastern world and save the Egyptian nation from famine. Joseph impressed Pharaoh and all his officials.

> Then Pharaoh said to Joseph, "Since God has made all this known to you, there is no one so discerning and wise as you. You shall be in charge of my palace, and all my people are to submit to your orders. Only with respect to the throne will I be greater than you."
>
> Genesis 41:39–40

Joseph had no guarantee that believing in God and trusting him through the challenges of his life would bring him reward. There is no guarantee that turning to God will earn you anything more than peace within the circumstances you are in. But what do you have to lose, except anger, bitterness, and depression? The key is not to have a self-directed positive attitude, but to have a God-centered love and trust from which a true positive attitude flows. Then like Joseph you can trust whether you are in the power seat or in prison. Joseph experienced major crises that were unfair and undeserved. Yet because he chose joy, his life was used dramatically by God. Do you feel you have been knocked down and trampled? How blessed you will be if you act as Joseph did—centering on what you do have, as opposed to what you do not have, and growing from your mistakes.

Paul: Direct Confrontation

God chiseled away the rough edges of Paul quite dramatically as compared to the slow, laborious method he used to polish Joseph. Paul was intelligent, headstrong, a leader, a man who took the reins and ran. He loved God but was far too busy delivering the radical members of the Way to justice to listen for God's guidance. To get Paul's attention God struck him down on the way to persecute more of the Christian-Jews. He blinded him and spoke directly.

> Meanwhile, Saul was still breathing out murderous threats against the Lord's disciples. . . .
>   As he neared Damascus on his journey, suddenly a light from heaven flashed around him. He fell to the ground and heard a voice say to him, "Saul, Saul, why do you persecute me?"
>
> Acts 9:1–4

Paul could have rebelled, though it is hard to turn your back on a direct experience where God speaks. He made a turnaround to commit his life to Christ. Was his life easy after that? Look at Paul's own evaluation of his difficulties:

I have worked much harder, been in prison more frequently, been flogged more severely, and been exposed to death again and again. Five times I received from the Jews the forty lashes minus one. Three times I was beaten with rods, once I was stoned, three times I was shipwrecked, I spent a night and a day in the open sea, I have been constantly on the move. I have been in danger from rivers, in danger from bandits, in danger from my own countrymen, in danger from Gentiles; in danger in the city, in danger in the country, in danger at sea; and in danger from false brothers. I have labored and toiled and have often gone without sleep; I have known hunger and thirst and have often gone without food; I have been cold and naked. Besides everything else, I face daily the pressure of my concern for all the churches.

2 Corinthians 11:23–28

No amount of travail could touch the joy Paul felt in knowing and having a personal relationship with God through Christ. Paul became God's instrument to bring change to the world as he shared Christ's message. Free your life to God's power so God can use you to change your world!

Ruth: Quiet Trust

Ruth was a caring, responsible young woman from Moab who centered her eyes on God's love through the difficult choices of her life. The Moabites were descended from Lot and his elder daughter and had been enemies of Israel while the tribes were in the wilderness. During a famine in Judah, an Israeli family—Elimelech, Naomi, and their two sons, Mahlon and Kilion—sought refuge in Moab. Ruth married Kilion, an unacceptable marriage in Moabite or Israeli culture.

Within ten years, Elimelech, Mahlon, and Kilion died, leaving Naomi and her two daughters-in-law widows.

Naomi determined to return to family in Bethlehem, and encouraged her two daughters-in-law to stay in their native country. She knew they would be unwelcome and estranged with a very slim chance of remarriage in Judah. Being widowed as a young woman is difficult. Ruth put aside her self-concerns to assume responsibility for her mother-in-law Naomi.

Ruth's devotion shone through her sunny disposition. Boaz, a wealthy landowner, fell in love with the radiant young woman from Moab and they married, changing Ruth's life direction and fulfilling God's design for Ruth to become the great-grandmother of the greatest king of Israel, David. All of us have the potential to be like Ruth. Our lives may not be a series of dramatic highs or lows as we face the challenges of life. If we walk as Ruth did, looking to God, he will polish us gently as we count our blessings instead of our difficulties.

Abraham: Gradual Growth

Abraham's diamond chiseling lessons came through a course of great financial and leadership successes combined with major failures. Like all of us, he did many things right and blew other opportunities royally. The life lesson that finally brought him to his knees was gleaned through failing to trust God's promise of a son by his beloved wife Sarah. Abraham took her handmaiden, Hagar, as his concubine; Ishmael was born from their union. Ishmael was Abraham's only son until, miracle of miracles, his aged, beloved wife, Sarah, conceived and bore Isaac.

After Isaac's birth Sarah railed against Abraham, "Get rid of that slave woman and her son, for that slave woman's son will never share in the inheritance with my son Isaac" (Gen. 21:10). Knowing the conflict that existed between Sarah and Hagar, Abraham could have established his first son, Ishmael, in another community. After all, Ishmael was a young man, and with his father's wealth and his mother's guidance, he would have felt loved and cherished by his father, even in another community while the immediate family bickering was settled. He could have provided Hagar and Ishmael safe conduct through the desert and money for their lifetime care. Instead, he banished them from the tribe with only a bag of food and water.

> Early the next morning Abraham took some food and a skin of water and gave them to Hagar. He set them on her shoulders and then sent her off with the boy. She went on her way and wandered in the desert of Beersheba.
>
> When the water in the skin was gone, she put the boy under one of the bushes. Then she went off and sat down nearby, about a bowshot away, for she thought, "I cannot watch the boy die." And as she sat there nearby, she began to sob.
>
> Genesis 21:14–16

No escort. No camels loaded with goods. No guide. Abraham sent his first child off in a moment of utter despair and distress. No one in a desert culture sends

---

Trusting in God is the joy choice!

---

someone into the desert with only a skin of water unless he is at his wit's end! From only son to exile, no wonder Ishmael, who became the father of the Arab nation, created a root of bitterness and strife that has divided the Arab and Jewish world from that point in history.

Abraham learned through this family tragedy to trust God completely, after a lifetime of partial commitment. He learned that God is a God who keeps his promises. Evidence of Abraham's growth is seen in his willingness to offer his beloved son Isaac for sacrifice. Through the complete submission of his will to God, Abraham became a priceless diamond.

God Has Great Blessings for You

Your life is as important to God as was Joseph's, Paul's, Ruth's, Abraham's, or any other person that has lived on this earth. Christ said, "I have come that they may have life, and that they may have it more abundantly" (John 10:10 NKJV). God's desire for our lives is that we be abundantly joy-filled. Why, then, does he allow difficult things to happen to us? Why doesn't God just make life easy? God allows difficulties because through them we grow and experience his blessings.

> We also rejoice in our sufferings, because we know that suffering produces perseverance; perseverance, character; and character, hope. And hope does not disappoint us, because God has poured out his love into our hearts by the Holy Spirit, whom he has given us.
>
> Romans 5:3–5

Receiving blessings is not dependent on what we have done in the past; it is dependent on what we do in the present. Doing what is right is dependent on our growing deep roots in the soil of trust so that we can forgive the mistakes, enjoy the successes, and rest in the knowledge that as long as we are here, God is chiseling us into his diamonds.

Going on a Journey

When I was in graduate school my dream was to earn a doctorate degree, or maybe even several doctorate degrees. I loved to learn and knew what I wanted. My ship was set on a direct course. Then my first child, Kim, was born, and our needs and life demands began to redirect my course. When a second child, Paul Edward, arrived three years later, I began to wonder at the miracle of the two little lives God had brought into my world. Paul and I were in school, residency, and military before we moved with our two little ones to a beautiful university city nestled in the mountain-lake area of Tennessee. Johnson City felt wonderfully stable, settled, and secure, though on occasion I reflected on and longed for what I perceived I had given up as our ship sailed in a very different direction from my original charted course.

Our last two children, Brad and LeeAnne, were born at a time in my life when my time, energy, love, and skill at teaching wed in the career of wife and mother. I was totally involved, fulfilled, and happy watching my children grow and develop. Life was wonderfully full of laughter and sunshine. Then unexpectedly and suddenly, a storm hit, threatening our ship's safety. We were thrown pell-mell into the world of medical needs when LeeAnne became diabetic at the age of two.

The storm brought blessings in disguise: Our family bonded as we worked together to handle the medical demands of our youngest daughter. We learned the fragility of health and the preciousness of each moment. Then suddenly, LeeAnne was gone. When she died there was a gaping hole in our lives. Our ship was aground. All the demands, needs, and care she required were gone. The laughter and giggles were silent. The joy that comes from being needed so critically evaporated. Beached, we slowly began to discover that God had strewn our world with flowers through the outreach of many friends and caregivers, flowers that brightened our hurting hearts and had not been a part of our sailing experience.

LeeAnne used to throw back her head in laughter, crying out, "Mom, aren't we lucky?!" Her boat had certainly
hit rocks, yet she felt such warming joy. We are all lucky!
We are blessed to be alive, to be able to smell the flowers,
to experience life even with our limitations and failures,
to be who we are and where we are. I don't know anyone
whose trip ends where he or she expected it to when the
journey began. But I do know with your trust planted
firmly in God, you are on a glorious voyage! Bon voyage!

Questions

1. Why is life so hard? Why doesn't God just make it
   easy?
2. How do you keep enthusiasm and zest as you live
   life?
3. What is the key that brings trust? Use a Bible character to illustrate trust in the midst of challenge.
4. Why does a Christian have no need to throw away
   the past?
5. What are the four different ways God polishes us?
   Give examples.
6. Why does God test us? Explain through Abraham's
   life.
7. Are you on the life trip you thought you were going
   to take?
8. Do you want to be happy? What is stopping you?

Diamonds

◊ *Seeing each moment of life as a gift frees our
   spirit to soar with enthusiasm.*
◊ *The past offers us great grow-up lessons.*

◊ *God polishes those who choose to trust him through their own unique experiences.*

◊ *Love brings trust; trust brings joy.*

◊ *You can decide to be happy, no matter where you have been or the time you have wasted.*

◊ *Trust in God gives us roots to hold us upright as we experience life.*

◊ *Trusting in God is the joy choice!*